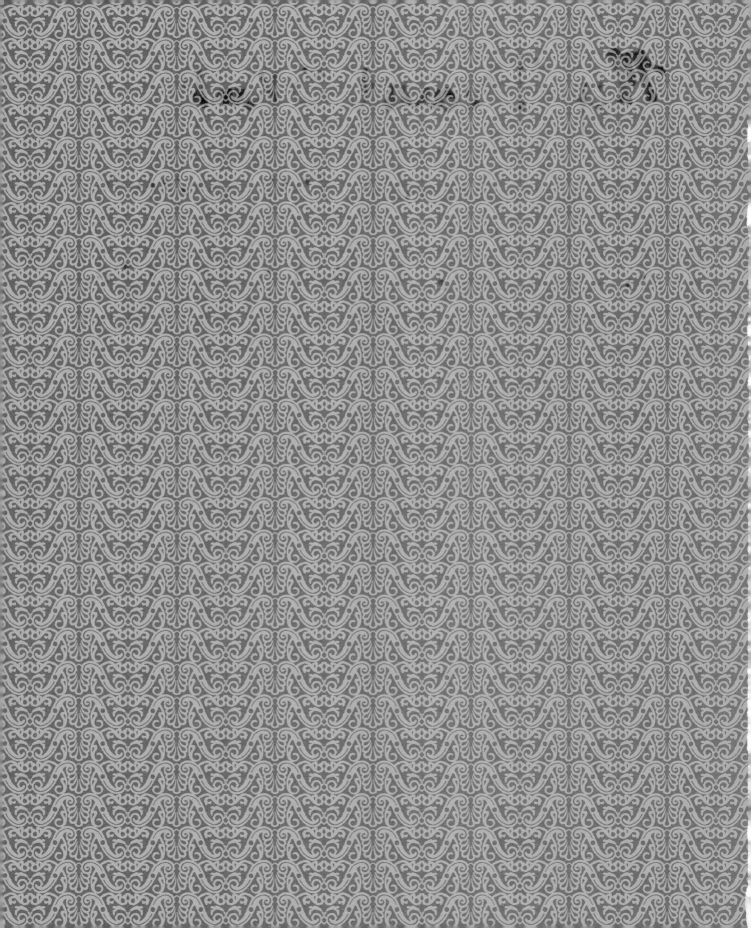

MARILYN
in FASHION

THE ENDURING INFLUENCE OF
MARILYN MONROE

CHRISTOPHER NICKENS
AND GEORGE ZENO

RUNNING PRESS
PHILADELPHIA · LONDON

My Dearest Sarah,

This is probably my favorite Marilyn book! Enjoy it, and think of me everything you open it! I left some notes for you ———

XoXo
Zach

Published by Running Press,
A Member of the Perseus Books Group

Printed in China

Books published by Running Press are available at special discounts for bulk purchases in the United States by corporations, institutions, and other organizations. For more information, please contact the Special Markets Department at the Perseus Books Group, 2300 Chestnut Street, Suite 200, Philadelphia, PA 19103, or call (800) 810-4145, ext. 5000, or e-mail special.markets@perseusbooks.com.

ISBN 978-0-7624-4332-1
Library of Congress Control Number: 2011938030

E-book ISBN 978-0-7624-4510-3

9 8 7 6 5 4 3 2 1
Digit on the right indicates the number of this printing

Designed by Corinda Cook
Edited by Cindy De La Hoz
Typography: Helvetica Neue and Requiem

Running Press Book Publishers
2300 Chestnut Street
Philadelphia, PA 19103-4371

Visit us on the web!
www.runningpress.com

FOR JAMES GALEANO
C. N.

AND FOR

ALEJANDRINA, VILMA, AND PETER,
WITH LOVE AND AFFECTION
G. Z.

CONTENTS

SEXUAL ELEGANCE 6

BECOMING MARILYN 14

PART ONE: THE DESIGNERS 24

   OLEG CASSINI 26

   CEIL CHAPMAN 32

   DOROTHY JEAKINS 42

   ELOIS JENSSEN 50

   CHARLES LEMAIRE 56

   DON LOPER 64

   JEAN LOUIS 68

JOHN MOORE 82

NORMAN NORELL 100

ORRY-KELLY 108

EMILIO PUCCI 114

RENIÉ 122

WILLIAM TRAVILLA 136

MISCELLANEOUS DESIGNERS 174

UNKNOWN DESIGNERS 184

PART TWO: A FASHIONABLE MISCELLANY 188

THE MAKEUP DEPARTMENT 190

THE HAIR SALON 200

TOPPING IT OFF 212

KEEPING COZY 226

MARILYN IN ENGLAND 232

OFF THE RACK 238

OUT OF THE CLOSET 246

SLACKS & JAX 254

SWEATER GIRL 264

PHOTOGRAPHY CREDITS 274

INDEX 275

ACKNOWLEDGMENTS 280

SEXUAL
ELEGANCE

ANYONE WHO EXAMINES MARILYN MON-
ROE'S LEGENDARY LIFE, EVEN A BIT, SOON
KNOWS THAT SHE WAS A COMPELLING
TANGLE OF CONTRADICTIONS. A UNIQUE
blend of qualities made her an unforgettable talent and
a captivating public personality. They also, of course,
shaped her fashion profile.

She was very much of the 1950s zeitgeist yet simul-
taneously years ahead of her time. She possessed a
reassuring ultra-feminine, girl-next-door sweetness
that coexisted with an almost supernatural sexual mag-
netism. This contrary blend made Monroe perfect for
a period that still cherished tradition, while slowly
moving into more openness about sex. In a time of
prim Peter Pan collars, voluminous skirts worn over
mountains of petticoats, and rubberized foundation
garments, Monroe was a style visionary whose fashion-
forward choices have transcended any specific era.
More than any other public figure of her time, she
brought body-conscious designs to the forefront in a
way that inspired countless designers, including Yves
St. Laurent, Alexander McQueen, Thierry Mugler, and
Jean Paul Gaultier.

Marilyn often anticipated the future. She went sans
undergarments years before the braless look became
acceptable. Thirty years prior to the fitness craze, she
was training with weights to maintain her stunning
figure. "It helps me keep what I've got where it
belongs," she quipped. Decades before "morning after"
hair was considered stylish, Monroe preferred a
tousled mane that contrasted dramatically with the
severe bobs favored by many of her peers. When she
had to don underwear for a see-through design, she
took the exotic step of wearing a stripper's G-string—
long before the invention of the thong.

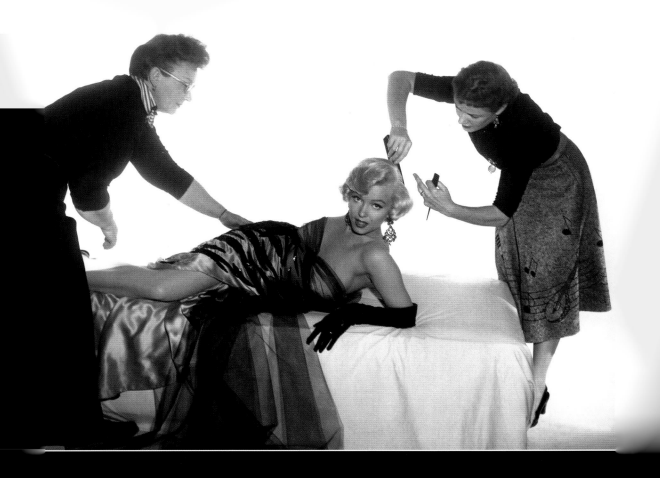

She also inspired trends. A bare-midriff cocktail dress she wore for a press reception in London was copied and rushed into stores, and the style lines of the iconic white dress she wore over the subway grating in *The Seven Year Itch* have been mimicked every spring since 1955.

Still, relatively little has been written about the powerful and lasting imprint Monroe has made on the world of fashion. Unlike Audrey Hepburn and Grace Kelly, commonly praised as the most influential style queens of mid-century Hollywood, Marilyn's standing took a while to be recognized. For years her built-in sensuality, voluptuous figure, and provocative taste worked against her being taken seriously by most fashion critics. Moreover, even when she appeared admirably chic, almost no one paid attention to the designer names responsible.

This was many years before anyone was shouting, "Who are you wearing?" on the red carpet. It was also a time when on-scene reporters and photographers were nearly all male. They were too busy jockeying for position to ask La Monroe about her style choices, even if they had been inclined to do so. Marilyn seldom revealed the identity of her fashion collaborators. She didn't want to hear, "What a gorgeous gown

Who designed it?" She much preferred "You look gorgeous!" Thus, it usually surprises fashionistas to learn that she wore the designs of Oleg Cassini, Hattie Carnegie, Ceil Chapman, Christian Dior, James Galanos, Lanvin, Don Loper, Norman Norell, and Emilio Pucci. She carried Louis Vuitton bags and wore Ferragamo pumps. She also shared America's top hairstylist with Jacqueline Kennedy.

On film, Marilyn was dressed exquisitely by Oscar-winning designers Jean Louis, William Travilla, Orry-Kelly, Charles LeMaire, and Dorothy Jeakins, among others. These artisans also had tremendous influence on Marilyn's off-screen image. She frequently took advantage of these designers as her personal couturiers, wearing their costumes off the studio lot for highly publicized events, or having them whip something up for her personal use. She was sheathed in a daring Jean Louis gown when she famously crooned "Happy Birthday" to President Kennedy.

Before style trends became as sexualized as they did later, fashion pundits tended to criticize Marilyn's "obvious" taste rather than salute her boldness—though sometimes they had a point. She did err occasionally on the side of vulgarity early in her career (when she had to stand out from the rest of the starlet pack), but she almost always managed to blend elegance with her ripe sexuality. The exhibitionist in her relished showing off as much of her magnificent body as the law allowed, but her need for respect led her to pair shocking décolleté with ladylike, opera-length gloves.

In a 1953 article entitled "I Dress for Men," Monroe shared her fashion philosophy. "I believe your body should make your clothes look good—instead of using clothes to make the body conform to what is considered fashionable at the moment, distorted or not. That's why I don't care for 'un-organic clothes'—clothes that have no relation to the body. Clothes, it seems to me, should have a relationship to the body, not be something distinct from it."

As she transitioned from a wholesome clean-scrubbed model to a sizzling Hollywood sexpot to an elegantly sexy living legend, Monroe refined her persona and set beauty standards that still resonate fifty years after her untimely death.

"Decades before stars would not make a public appearance without the services of platoons of stylists and designers," wrote British journalist Meredith Etherington-Smith, "Marilyn was a truly great stylist. She knew exactly how to get the effect she wanted with black jersey, fine silk-crepe, or a solid nimbus of skin-tight sequins."

In 1992 *The New York Times* called Monroe "Timeless Marilyn, the Movies' Mona Lisa." This characterization is stronger than ever twenty years later. Coinciding with the release of *My Week with Marilyn* in 2011, The *New York Post* headlined "Dress Like Marilyn," a two-page photo layout featuring updates on familiar Monroe outfits.

Of course, Marilyn's hair and makeup styles have proved irresistible for decades, showing up on everyone from Jayne Mansfield to Kelly Osbourne, from Madonna to Christina Aguilera, from Anna Nicole Smith to Gwen Stefani. Nearly every year magazine tutorials appear on how to replicate Marilyn's perfectly arched brows, glistening lips, or one of her signature hairdos—styles from sixty years in the past! Featured in advertising promotions for Sunsilk hair products in 2008, Marilyn was pictured alongside Madonna and Shakira as if she were their contemporary. "She never seems to really die," marveled Liz Smith in 2010.

Why Marilyn Monroe continues unabated to hold generation after generation in thrall, why auctions of her personal effects fetch upwards of seven figures, why she continues to inspire designers, stylists, and some of the world's most exciting women is a subject that could fill a book all its own. In terms of fashion it can be summed up easily: She was a stylish girl ahead of her time that became a style icon for all time.

BECOMING
MARILYN

The dramatic transformation that Norma Jeane Dougherty* underwent to become Marilyn Monroe lasted, on and off, for five years. It has long been proposed that it was wholly the creation of an efficient platoon of Hollywood magicians. Though there is some truth to that, no one worked harder than Marilyn herself at honing the beauty that would set timeless glamour standards. From the moment she first smiled into a professional photographer's lens, she embarked on a quest for self-improvement that would encompass far more than her looks.

For someone with little formal education, and despite the public confusing her with her award-winning portrayals of dumb blondes, Marilyn was intelligent, ambitious, shrewd, innately talented, and always eager to learn. Her intelligence led her to soak up knowledge like a sponge from mentors she admired and trusted.

*Pinning down Marilyn's pre-professional name is a challenge. She was born Norma Jeane Mortenson, baptized Norma Jeane Baker, and in school, as a typical teenager, she experimented; losing the Mortenson entirely, often dropping the "e" from Jeane, and even going by Norma on occasion. With her first marriage at sixteen, she became Norma Jeane Dougherty from 1944 through 1947, when she was christened Marilyn Monroe.

16^{98} PLUS POSTAGE

Sensationally new! Smart styling makes it perfect to wear anywhere. 100% wool Shetland fabric gives it that "always fresh" look. Jacket is fully rayon lined. Gored skirt has taped hems and a metal zipper. Four beautiful pastel shades from which to choose. Jackets have contrasting color inserts in front. Sizes 10 to 20.

———————★———————

SEND NO MONEY — WE WILL MAIL C. O. D.

———————★———————

TRY AT OUR RISK — If you are not perfectly satisfied every cent you have paid will be refunded to you immediately.

———————★———————

Arnold's of Hollywood

Dept. A1, 5205 Hollywood Blvd., Hollywood 27, Calif.

In the December 1945 issue of *Movieland*, the future Marilyn Monroe is seen in a movie magazine for the first time. She is modeling a remarkably priced suit made of "100% wool Shetland fabric." The name of the suit, and the fact that it is advertised in such a magazine, might suggest a prophecy, and perhaps it was.

When Norma Jeane was still a scrawny kid bouncing from one dreary foster home to another in blue-collar neighborhoods of Los Angeles, she loved going to the movies at Grauman's Chinese Theatre in Hollywood. Grace McKee, a family friend, often accompanied her. Known as something of a reliable fortuneteller, Grace once told the girl, "Don't worry, Norma Jeane. You're going to be a beautiful girl when you get big. You're going to be an important woman. You're going to be a movie star. Oh, I feel it in my bones."

Marilyn was born in Los Angeles on June 1, 1926. Her unwed parents were Gladys Baker, a mentally challenged, inconsistent presence in her daughter's life, and Edward Mortenson, an absentee father from day one. When she was able to work, Gladys labored as a film cutter for the studios. To help survive her miserable childhood, Norma Jeane did indeed entertain fantasies of movie stardom. At nine she was going to Vine Street Elementary School and living in the nearby Los Angeles Orphan's Home. Before bedtime, she would stare wistfully out a window at the tall RKO Studios sign two blocks away and think, "My mother used to work there. Someday I'd like to be a star there."

When she posed for this ad, however, she was just happy to be earning some decent money. She had only been modeling for a matter of weeks. She was nineteen and working for $35 a week at the Radio Plane Factory in Burbank when photographer David Conover spotted her on the assembly line. For the next couple of weeks, Conover took several rolls of film of Norma Jeane. He said later he was captivated by "a luminous quality in her face, a fragility combined with astonishing vibrancy."

With her flawless complexion, large blue/grey eyes, and dazzling smile, Norma Jeane embodied the wholesome girl next door. Conover soon recommended her to other photographers, and they in turn suggested she try her luck at the city's top modeling agency.

At the Ambassador Hotel in Los Angeles, Norma Jeane, second from left, poses in 1946 with other girls represented by the Blue Book Model Agency. Her sundress in shades of blue is backless with a draped halter neck and a midriff-baring bodice attached to a loosely pleated skirt. The dress (which is similar to the styles Norma Jeane favored for her personal wardrobe) was courtesy of the nearby Bullocks Wilshire department store. It is often assumed that Marilyn spent most of her modeling career in various states of undress. And while it's true that the volume of published cheesecake poses over the next year led to her first Hollywood contract, she took many early assignments in which she promoted fashions that could hardly be called provocative.

Emmeline Snively, doyenne of the Blue Book agency, became Monroe's first style and beauty guide. Initially, she felt Norma Jeane was hopelessly shy and resembled a "cherub in a church choir," but she saw a natural sensuality in the girl that was relatively easy to train into genuine modeling talent. Norma Jeane had been attracting wolf whistles since early puberty. By this time, she was well aware of the power her looks had, especially on men. Exploiting that power within a professional setting made sense to her.

She applied herself at Blue Book as if she were on scholarship at Harvard. She realized that modeling could lead to a much bigger life if she took full advantage of this opportunity that had fallen into her lap. "She gobbled up every bit of instruction," Snively told *Modern Screen* in 1954. "She was wonderful on hand positions, body positions, and simply great when it came to makeup."

One of the first things Snively noticed was that Norma Jeane's upper gum line showed a bit when she laughed. She advised her to lower her lip line whenever she smiled. Marilyn spent hours in front of the mirror until she had perfected the move, but she remained conscious of the artifice for years. This maneuver may be the cause of the quivery lips that critics poked fun at in her early movies. Still, for the rest of her life, when Marilyn was caught off guard and burst out laughing, her gums would show.

MARILYN IN FASHION

Snively also saw to it that Norma Jeane underwent electrolysis to clean up her hairline, which brought out her dramatic widow's peak. The most important suggestion Snively made, however, didn't go over well with Norma Jeane at first. She wanted her to lighten her hair, which photographed darker than its sable brown. (Norma Jeane had been blonde as a little girl, but as often happens, her hair darkened after a few years). "I didn't want to be a bleached blonde," Marilyn said later. Snively sent her to color expert Sylvia Barnhart at the Frank & Joseph's salon on Hollywood Boulevard, where her hair was straightened and lightened. When Norma Jeane saw how much more work she got as a blonde, she grew comfortable with the new honey-colored shade. She had no way of knowing at the time that within a couple of years, she would be *the* blonde in a town awash with peroxide.

A week after her twenty-second birthday in 1948, the newly named Marilyn Monroe is photographed at a Hollywood party with veteran entertainer George Jessel. This is the first time she was seen with a shorter hairstyle, and within a few months she would have it styled into a sleeker version for her important breakthrough role in *The Asphalt Jungle* at MGM.

It was around this time that Marilyn met Johnny Hyde, a powerful agent, who became her lover and crucial to her rise to fame. It was Hyde who sponsored the minor cosmetic surgery Marilyn underwent. She had the tip of her nose shortened, and later her nostrils narrowed. In a third procedure, a small piece of cartilage was added to the right side of her chin to even out her jaw line.

Thanks to Hyde's connections and deep pockets, he had access to the best doctors for these subtle alterations. So many actresses at the time underwent cookie cutter "nose jobs" that could be spotted a block away. Hyde had managed plenty of lovely starlets, but he felt instinctively that Marilyn had something very special. "You're going to be a great movie star," he told her more than once. "Just Wait..."

In May 1950, Marilyn sits for this pleasingly natural portrait that is free of affectation. She was several months away from signing her second and lasting contract with Twentieth Century Fox.

By the time she achieved stardom two years later, she had perfected an arsenal of facial expressions to convey a myriad of moods. With her head tilted back, eyelids lowered and lips moist and parted she sent a clear message of sexual availability. Larger than life exuberance was expressed with an open-mouthed smile that showed off her perfect teeth, and a wide-eyed "who me?" look brought to mind the innocence of a child. Marilyn finessed these expressions (and many others, of course) so naturally that they became organic. Soon, every starlet in Hollywood was being encouraged to copy Monroe's poses, but none succeeded with the same impact.

BECOMING MARILYN

THOSE. EYES.

Around the time of *Ladies of the Chorus* filming in 1948, Marilyn posed for a photo series illustrating various exercises she liked. As her sex appeal became a more pronounced component of her image—particularly after her sultry exchange with Groucho Marx in *Love Happy*—she took up a regimen of calisthenics, stretching, and even weight lifting to keep her body toned. Early mornings found her jogging in the wide alleys of Beverly Hills.

Also in 1949, Marilyn posed nude for photographer Tom Kelley. She needed to raise money for her rent or a car payment, depending on which story one believes. Though tasteful, the photos would come back to haunt her in the form of a calendar just as she was approaching stardom.

When Marilyn sat for this pouty portrait in 1951 to publicize *Clash By Night*, all the tinkering with her looks was complete, and her career was about to ignite in a huge way. Much analysis over the years has centered on the Norma Jeane-to-Marilyn transition and the psychological impact it had on the ambitious but emotionally sensitive young girl at its center. In truth, what Marilyn underwent was quite common among Hollywood hopefuls of both sexes. Psychological impact aside, Marilyn's alterations were minor compared to what many other young aspirants had to undergo.

PART ONE

THE
DESIGNERS

OLEG CASSINI

(1913–2006)

RUSSIAN BORN OLEG CASSINI STUDIED IN PARIS, SKETCHED FOR PATOU, AND WON SEVERAL FASHION COMPETITIONS IN MILAN BEFORE MOVING TO THE UNITED STATES. He became an assistant to designer Edith Head at Paramount Studios in the late 1930s. Cassini married glamorous actress Gene Tierney in 1941, acquired American citizenship, and served in the Army during World War II. He was Tierney's exclusive movie designer until their divorce in 1953. Cassini basked in the limelight and enjoyed being playful. He titled one of his designs that featured a bare midriff, "Navel Operations."

Cassini's greatest fame came in 1961 when Jacqueline Kennedy—a friend of longstanding—appointed him official couturier for her reign as First Lady. Defined by unfussy lines, high crew necklines, suits that were stripped down versions of Chanel and pillbox hats, the "Jackie Look," as dictated by Cassini in over three hundred outfits, became the most influential fashion profile of the era.

MARILYN BY CASSINI

In January 1952, Marilyn starred in her first fashion controversy when she made this entrance at the Club Del Mar in Santa Monica. She was being honored with a Henrietta Award as "Best Young Box Office Personality" by a group of journalists who had split off from the Hollywood Foreign Press Association.

This velvet fishtail style gown in a deep garnet was designed by Cassini for Gene Tierney to wear in *Where the Sidewalk Ends*. On Tierney, the basket-weave sweetheart neckline was held up with a right-side shoulder strap consisting of several rope-like pieces that echoed the basket weave. "That dress is dangerous!" declared Tierney's director, Otto Preminger. When Tierney was offered the gown to keep, she declined, saying that it was so tight she couldn't walk six feet in it.

Marilyn bought the gown at Cassini's private salon and chose to wear it with the shoulder strap tucked away. She also made sure the chocolate mink stole she added for this occasion did nothing to conceal her daringly exposed chest. Photographers hovered around her all night hoping for a glimpse of nipple, but miraculously that didn't happen. Still, photos of Marilyn with her nearly bare chest hit newspapers the next day, inspiring a scolding from conservative columnists.

Though she was by then the most talked-about starlet in movies, Marilyn knew she had to still set herself apart from the army of other young beauties vying for attention in Hollywood. She

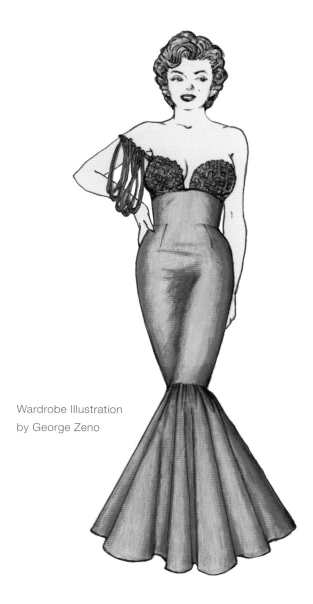

Wardrobe Illustration
by George Zeno

learned quickly how to mix sex and fashion, and her rethinking of this Cassini design is a typical result. The gown itself was slightly provocative, but Monroe figured out a way to make it shocking, and the resulting publicity naturally increased her name value.

Commenting on the design, Marilyn told *Modern Screen*, "I've always admired [Cassini's] taste and imagination in women's clothes, and my gown is no exception. It fits snugly down to my knees and then flares out, in the Lillian Russell tradition." With a straight face she added, "It plunges somewhat in the front, but not extremely." One fan magazine declared the gown "the most risqué design of the year."

A year later, Monroe donned the gown for this luscious publicity portrait, once again dropping the shoulder strap.

The second Cassini/Tierney cast off Marilyn made the most of is this floor-length evening gown in fire-engine red jersey. The bodice is in a graceful pin-tuck style. Ruching down the back creates a snug fit to below the left hip. Encircling the right hip below the waist is a sash of royal purple that ties in a knot before cascading to the floor with the full skirt. Gene Tierney wore the gown in *On the Riviera*, a 1951 musical comedy with Danny Kaye.

Here Marilyn wears the *On the Riviera* dress in September 1952 as her hair is subjected to a curling iron prior to the premiere of *Monkey Business*, held at the Stanley Theatre in Atlantic City.

"I saw clearly the qualities that would later make Marilyn Monroe so successful," wrote Oleg Cassini, "the sweetness, the vulnerability, the curious triple-edged naivete, at once innocent, encouraging, and gently mocking. This was not just a body walking around, there was a brain attached."

OLEG CASSINI

"What's your favorite scary Movie?"

CEIL CHAPMAN

CEIL CHAPMAN* BEGAN HER DESIGNING/ MANUFACTURING CAREER IN HER NATIVE NEW YORK IN 1940. After a brief business partnership with Gloria Vanderbilt she established the *Ladyship Gowns* line. A decade later she was known as the nation's "#1 glamour dress designer," famous for sexy "bombshell" cocktail dresses and breezy daywear in striking prints.

Elizabeth Taylor's trousseau for her 1950 marriage to Nicky Hilton consisted of Chapman pieces, and the designer later supplied a wedding dress for Mamie Van Doren. (Chapman was the only designer to have dressed Marilyn Monroe and her two most prominent look-alikes, Van Doren and Jayne Mansfield).

For her fall 1957 line, Ceil Chapman was one of the first fashion stars to reintroduce (from the 1930s) the use of the bias cut, called by *Women's Wear Daily* "certainly one of the softest and most flattering treatments of fabrics ever." Chapman was also known for her ability to drape and twist fabric for maximum figure-flattering results.

*Even *The New York Times* couldn't unearth Ceil Chapman's birth date, and her death is reported as having occurred "sometime in the 1970s."

MARILYN BY CHAPMAN

In 1950, Marilyn models a black crepe cocktail dress with the single shoulder strap balanced by a Chapman trademark, a gathering of fabric onto the opposite hip, topped by a rosette. Opera-length gloves add sophistication.

CEIL CHAPMAN

When renowned photographer Philippe Halsman turned up at Marilyn's Hollywood apartment for a *Life* magazine shoot in early 1952, he was surprised at her paltry wardrobe. Fortunately she came up with this Chapman floor-length gown of off-white crepe. Ruching at the hips and sleeves give it a somewhat classical style—perfect for an emerging movie goddess. As was her wont, Monroe pulled the dress off her shoulders.

Halsman was unimpressed with a shy Marilyn the first time he photographed her three years earlier. After this shoot he marveled, "I know of few actresses who have this incredible talent for communicating with a camera lens. She would try to seduce a camera as if it were a human being." An alternate from this sitting brought Marilyn her first *Life* magazine cover on April 7, 1952.

As Grand Marshall of the Miss America Pageant in Atlantic City in September 1952, Marilyn agreed to countless photo opportunities, including this one with Miss Alabama. The summery Chapman dress is ivory rayon with oversized red polka dots. The square neckline was low cut but not objectionable until Marilyn posed with a group of women in uniform from various branches of the armed forces. For that shot, a photographer jumped on a chair (or aimed from a balcony depending on which story one prefers), and the Monroe cleavage he captured from that angle caused a ruckus. Armed forces public relations sought to kill the photograph, which of course, only called attention to it. Even though this particular wardrobe controversy wasn't Marilyn's fault, she reacted defensively. "You would think all other women kept their bodies in vaults," she said. Typical of the times, few thought to ask who designed the dress at the center of this brouhaha.

CEIL CHAPMAN

That DRESS!

Joe DiMaggio and his fiancé pose with General William F. Dean during a Hollywood charity fundraiser in 1953. Marilyn described her cocktail dress to *Modern Screen* as "black silk by Ceil Chapman which has a big puff at the side and drapes tightly around my legs. I like its slimming effect."

While she was on her honeymoon in Japan, Marilyn was asked by the U.S.O. to make a detour to Korea to entertain the fighting men. She readily agreed. She knew she was the number-one pinup of the Korean conflict and had been trying for two years to clear her schedule for a trip to the war zone. For four days in mid-February 1954, she sang a handful of songs in ten shows at various bases in front of one hundred thousand cheering troops. "I never felt like a star before in my heart," Marilyn said of the experience. "It was so wonderful to look down and see a fellow smiling at me."

Because this whirlwind tour was impromptu, Marilyn had to make do with the wardrobe she brought on her honeymoon. She ended up performing in this cocktail dress made of crepe in a deep eggplant. The simple sheath style featured shoelace straps and was embroidered with tone-on-tone bugle beads set in a vermicular pattern. Tiny sequins were scattered over the fabric for added sparkle. Marilyn loved this design and had Chapman whip up one for her in black.

MARILYN IN FASHION

The dress had a matching long sleeved, bolero-length jacket, as seen here on Marilyn while she hammed it up with Dean Martin and Jerry Lewis in Hollywood a year earlier. Even though the temperatures in Korea were frigid, Marilyn seldom wore the jacket on stage. She knew the boys wanted to see as much skin as possible. Because of the news coverage of Monroe's Korean trip, this design became the most famous of Ceil Chapman's career. Decades later, Mariah Carey had a shorter duplicate made in chocolate.

In the summer of 1957, Arthur Miller and Marilyn attend a party at the Barbizon Plaza Theatre following a performance of Noel Coward's *Conversation Piece*. Greeting them is the play's star, Joan Copeland, Miller's sister. Monroe is in a cream cocktail dress with vermicular bugle beading. She opted for elegance with the matching elbow-length gloves, but she kept her hair slightly unkempt—a contradiction that she favored often.

Just prior to the start of filming *Some Like It Hot* in the summer of 1958, Marilyn is photographed in Hollywood with gossip queen Louella Parsons. The dress is sleeveless black satin. A panel of embroidered black lace forms a scoop neckline and then trails over the bodice to just below Marilyn's left hip. It is held in place by a brooch made up of tiny coral beads. This would be the last Ceil Chapman design that Marilyn would be photographed in.

DOROTHY JEAKINS

(1914–1995)

AFTER STUDYING AT THE OTIS ART INSTITUTE IN LOS ANGELES, SAN DIEGO-BORN DOROTHY JEAKINS SERVED AS A SKETCH ARTIST FOR THE WALT DISNEY STUDIOS IN THE 1930s. She then moved on to fashion design for I. Magnin's department store on Wilshire Boulevard. It was there in 1948 that she was discovered by director Victor Fleming. He hired her to collaborate with Barbara Karinska to design costumes for his Ingrid Bergman vehicle, *Joan of Arc*. To Jeakins' shock, she and Karinska won an Academy Award for their efforts—the first Oscar ever given for Costume Design.

Jeakins would go on to freelance for every studio in town for forty years, winning two more Oscars in the process. She created wardrobe for two Marilyn Monroe films, *Niagara* (1953) and *Let's Make Love* in 1960. She also designed for *The Ten Commandments*, *The Night of the Iguana*, *The Sound of Music*, *Young Frankenstein*, and *The Way We Were*.

MARILYN BY JEAKINS

March 1952: Marilyn is on the run after tossing out the first ball for the "Out of This World Series," a charity softball game at Gilmore Field in Los Angeles. The dress is a Jeakins design for *Niagara*. It is dusty pink, made of tropical wool. The turn-out collar and a row of buttons add interest to the simple halter top. Marilyn wore the dress for *Niagara* publicity photos but not in the film.

During a trip to New York the following August, Marilyn was interviewed wearing the dress for the *Journal American*. "On the coast," she said, "we could wear this dress out of doors. Here we wear it indoors. People are so conservative."

Though Monroe often posed for what might be described as aggressively seductive portraits, *Niagara* was the only film in which she played a classic predatory femme fatale. Jeakins' designs artfully delineated the wanton persona of Rose Loomis, Marilyn's character. On Rose, even tailored suits looked sexy.

Marilyn poses in the light magenta dress she wore to sing "Kiss," in the film's most famous scene. The Jeakins creation fairly screams "I'm available!" The low-cut top looks as if a tug on the bow would reveal Rose's breasts. The peek-a-boo midriff leads to a very unusual feature, a zipper that anyone bold enough could easily pull down! Much more sedate versions of this dress became popular retail items after the film was released.

Monroe wears the dress to a ballyhooed press party at the Hollywood hills home of bandleader Ray Anthony (at right in above photo) on August 3, 1952. She arrived by helicopter to publicize Anthony's new record, "Marilyn." She chatted with reporters from around the world and posed with attendees including Lassie and her old buddy, Mickey Rooney.

DOROTHY JEAKINS

This suit in pale turquoise dupion silk is another *Niagara* costume that Marilyn wore several times off screen. It may seem odd to think of stars wearing their movie wardrobe away from the soundstages, but it was done quite often. "People tend to equate movie costumes with theater clothes," says Greg Schriener, an expert on the subject, and the owner of a famous Monroe collection that includes several of her costumes. "Theater wardrobe is constructed to withstand constant wear and tear as it is changed frequently. Audiences see the costumes from a distance, so there is a lot of illusion involved.

"Film clothes, those worn by stars, must be precisely designed to fit beautifully and tailored so that every seam and hem will look flawless in a close-up. Fox, like every major studio, had only the most talented designers and tailors on staff. The clothes Marilyn wore from studio wardrobe were superbly crafted and fit her as if they were from a top designer's salon."

Another *Niagara* outfit consists of a loosely defined blouse worn under a wide-sleeved wool jacket with a notch collar, and an oversized single button. A snug black wool skirt completes the look. For the film, Marilyn added a square handbag in clear Lucite.

It was in this costume that the famous hip-gyrating "horizontal" Monroe walk was immortalized as she was filmed for more than twenty seconds of screen time walking away from the camera.

DOROTHY JEAKINS

A childhood dream comes true as Marilyn places her hand and footprints in wet cement in the forecourt of Grauman's Chinese Theatre in Hollywood on June 26, 1953. She shares the honor with Jane Russell, her costar in *Gentlemen Prefer Blondes*. Her white halter neck cotton sheath features eyelets and a contrasting sash in pink. It is likely that Jeakins also designed Russell's complementary dress for the occasion.

Marilyn appreciated Dorothy Jeakins' well thought-out designs for *Niagara*, but she was less thrilled with her *Let's Make Love* wardrobe seven year later. For her role as an entertainer in an intimate Greenwich Village musical comedy revue, Marilyn wore this black rehearsal costume. It is a bikini combined with theatrical tights and self-tie details. She topped it with a bulky blue sweater for her entrance into the film singing "My Heart Belongs to Daddy." This is one of only a handful of Jeakins designs that she ultimately approved. For two key scenes, Monroe wore two of her favorite John Moore designs from her personal wardrobe, a clear indication of her displeasure with Jeakins' designs.

Still, Jeakins was originally set to do Marilyn's clothes for *The Misfits*, which began production on the heels of *Let's Make Love*. In a March 3, 1960 letter to Monroe, Dorothy Jeakins wanly suggests that she be replaced. "I am sorry I have displeased you," she wrote. She suggests that if Marilyn doesn't care for her *Misfits* sketches, "someone else can then take over." Soon, Jean Louis did precisely that.

DOROTHY JEAKINS

ELOIS JENSSEN
(1922–2004)

CALIFORNIA NATIVE ELOIS JENSSEN STUDIED FASHION
DESIGN IN PARIS AND AT THE CHOUINARD ART INSTITUTE
IN LOS ANGELES. She began designing for film with *Dishonored Lady* in
1947, and shared an Academy Award with Edith Head, Dorothy Jeakins, Gile
Steele, and Gwen Wakeling for *Samson and Delilah* in 1949.

Following her sole Monroe picture, *We're Not Married* in 1952, Jenssen
turned to television, where she designed Lucille Ball's wardrobe for two seasons
of *I Love Lucy* and Ann Sothern's clothes for *Private Secretary*. Jenssen received
her second Academy Award nomination for her final film *Tron*, in 1982.

Marilyn is Annabel, a doll-like young bride in this Jenssen
design from *We're Not Married*. The mid-calf dress is of off-
white embroidered organza. A petal-edged capelet hugs
her shoulders and leads the eye to a sweetheart neckline.

MARILYN BY JENSSEN

This tailored sportswear from *We're Not Married* is a prime example of a studio costume that Marilyn requisitioned for her personal use. It is a buttoned-down shirtwaist in beige with contrasting buttons and dotted novelty trim. The short-sleeved cover-up features a shawl collar. The self-covered belt is an optional accessory. After the costume test, the skirt slit was modified and the hat was eliminated before the dress appeared on screen.

Monroe added gloves
when she wore it in
Atlantic City as part
of the Miss America
pageant festivities
she attended in
September 1952.

ELOIS JENSSEN

This swimsuit in black rayon features peek-a-boo cutouts on the sides of the hips with graduated criss-cross lacing, culminating in small bows that mimic the neckline. The spaghetti straps tie with small bows as well.

GOULDING A666
MARILYN MONROE
AS "ANNABEL"
CH #3
EXT. MISS
MISSISSIPPI
FINALS -
42 TO 46

DES. JENSSEN
1/11/52

Annabel wins the Miss Mississippi title in this elegant one-piece swim-suit. It is cream colored and boasts a paisley and scrolling graphic design embroidered in beads and metallic thread. Delicate scallop bordering sits above the lower hem.

Fans of Marilyn Monroe pinups will recognize the unusual platform heels. They are made of sturdy clear Lucite, threaded through with ribbon, which could be switched out for a color change. Marilyn wore the shoes in many of her cheesecake photo layouts as well as for a stunning entrance she makes in *How To Marry a Millionaire.* Modeling a red swimsuit trimmed with rhinestones, she wears the shoes with ribbons of matching color.

ELOIS JENSSEN

CHARLES LEMAIRE

(1897–1985)

AS A TEENAGER CHARLES LEMAIRE CREATED COSTUMES FOR VAUDE-VILLE PERFORMERS IN HIS NATIVE CHICAGO. He moved on to Broadway, where he designed for *The Ziegfeld Follies* before making Hollywood his home in 1925. Over the course of forty years, and more than two hundred films, he dressed everyone from silent star Barbara LaMarr to young Jane Fonda. By the late 1940s, LeMaire was wardrobe director at Twentieth Century Fox, where he oversaw (and often tweaked) every star costume on the lot as well as continuing to design on his own. He won three Academy Awards, including one for *All About Eve* in 1950.

MARILYN BY LEMAIRE

Cameraman Milton Krasner illuminates Marilyn in her role as an aspiring stage actress (known only as Miss Casswell) on the set of *All About Eve*. Her formal is a LeMaire design in ice-blue satin brocade and matching tulle. The bodice is ruched on the diagonal with an asymmetrical chording detail to Monroe's left hip where it meets a cluster of silk flowers. The full skirt dips from the hip diagonally across to below the right hip where it then drops to the floor. For her scene in the film, Marilyn wore a full-length white ermine wrap over the gown.

CHARLES LEMAIRE

March 29, 1951: Monroe poses backstage at the Pantages Theatre in Hollywood with Thomas Moulton, to whom she had just presented the Academy Award for Best Sound Recording for *All About Eve*. For this, her only appearance on an Oscar show (broadcast only on the radio) Marilyn wore an evening gown of black tulle. The extremely low-cut sweetheart neckline was obscured with a layer of tulle that could be worn up over the shoulders as seen here, or pulled down as Marilyn has done in the fashion shot on the opposite page. Clusters of sequins brightened up the many yards of fabric that made up the skirt.

Shortly before taking the stage, Marilyn noticed that the skirt was torn. She panicked and while Jane Greer, Debra Paget, and Gloria DeHaven soothed her nerves, a seamstress rushed over and repaired the damage. This gown was a hand-me-down, originally worn by Valentina Cortese in *The House on Telegraph Hill*, filmed several months before this event. Renié was the designer credited for the movie, but if LeMaire suggested the addition of even a single sequin, he would likely claim it as a collaboration. In that regard he was not unlike his counterpart at Paramount, Edith Head.

Mr. and Mrs. Joe DiMaggio emerge from their civil wedding ceremony in San Francisco on January 14, 1954. After a highly publicized courtship of two years, the baseball legend and the blonde bombshell were bound for a honeymoon in Japan.

Marilyn's buttoned-to-the neck, three-quarter length suit was of chocolate brown broadcloth, relieved only by a white ermine collar and simple brooch. Its demureness caused as much press comment as her daring necklines usually did. Where, reporters asked, was the customary Monroe oomph? Marilyn chose the suit in an effort to please her new husband, not the fourth estate. Joe didn't wholly approve of her sexpot image, so she felt dignity was the way to go for this special moment in her groom's hometown.

Writer Alice Hoffman accompanied Marilyn to San Francisco for the ceremony. In a subsequent article Hoffman wrote for *Modern Screen*, she established a myth about Monroe buying this suit at the last minute from Joseph Magnin's in Union Square.

MARILYN IN FASHION

Though she did buy some clothes at Magnin's, they were for her honeymoon. This suit is a Charles LeMaire design. Marilyn wore it two months earlier, in November 1953, when she greeted Greek royalty visiting the Fox lot.

The newlyweds are spotted at the San Francisco airport to grab a plane to Hawaii and then on to Japan. Marilyn is wearing another LeMaire suit with a small leopard-skin detail at the collar.

CHARLES LEMAIRE

Facing a small army of reporters and photographers in Japan, Monroe wears another LeMaire dress. It is in blue gabardine with a black collar trimmed in sequins and a detachable bow. A black mink coat gave it a dollop of glamour.

In Manhattan on September 12, 1954 the DiMaggios enjoy a night out at El Morocco. Three days later Marilyn filmed the subway grate scene for *The Seven Year Itch*, which hastened the dissolution of her marriage. She is wearing a LeMaire suit of black wool gabardine topped with a portrait collar. Monroe was not fond of most necklaces, but she sometimes chose another accessory for such designs. "I wear fresh red roses at the plunged neckline. I like to wear flowers; I even have some artificial ones for times when fresh ones aren't handy."

A year earlier in Hollywood, Marilyn, Esther Williams, and Esther's husband, Ben Gage, were seated together at a party. *Silver Screen* magazine captured an exchange between the couple: Esther observed, "In the 'v' of the neck of [Marilyn's low-cut dress] she wore a rose. It was supposed to cover the cleavage, but it didn't entirely." Gage noted, "That rose looks wilted." "Oh honey," Esther laughed, "it's burned to a crisp!"

(Left) In the same gabardine suit, with no roses, but a discreet strand of Mikimoto pearls (a gift from the Emperor of Japan), Marilyn is ladylike and glowing on October 22, 1954, as she receives a divorce decree from Joe DiMaggio in a Santa Monica court.

DON LOPER

(1906–1972)

HAILING FROM OHIO, DON LOPER MEANDERED INTO HIS DESIGNING CAREER AFTER LABORING IN STUDIO MUSIC DEPARTMENTS. AT FOX IN 1944, he served as choreographer for *Four Jills in a Jeep* and the Ginger Rogers vehicle *Lady in the Dark*. For a time, he was an assistant to musical producer Arthur Freed at MGM. He opened a swank dress salon on the Sunset Strip in 1946 that catered to Hollywood royalty and Pasadena society. In 1952 he designed Marlene Dietrich's costumes for Fritz Lang's offbeat western, *Rancho Notorious*. Other movie assignments were for *The Big Combo* and *Paris Follies of 1956*. Barbra Streisand called on Loper in 1964 to help fabricate her design for the black velvet gown she wore to the opening night party of her Broadway triumph in *Funny Girl*. Loper is best remembered, however, for playing himself on "The Fashion Show," an episode of *I Love Lucy* in 1955.

MARILYN BY LOPER

For a 1951 magazine layout, Marilyn models three Loper designs at his salon. This formal is in pale blue chiffon. The shoulder treatments feature decorative beadwork, and there is beading at the waist. There is further sparkle in a subtle scattering of beads placed under the top layer of the skirt. In the back, two long panels of the dress material descend from the shoulders. These could be worn flowing down the back or as a built-in wrap, as Marilyn indicates.

This dress in navy chiffon over lace is tea length with a self-belt. It has gauzy shoulders that square off an expanse of exposed chest and a modified sweetheart neckline. Low-heeled, open-toed black pumps call too much attention to themselves. The only Loper piece we know Marilyn owned for sure was a beige suit, but these designs were too conservative for her personal wardrobe. She models them, however, with decorum and only a hint of the sexiness that characterized so many of her photo layouts of the time.

A hostess gown of silk is in dusty rose with forest green elbow-length cuffs and accents on the stand up collar. The green follows the neckline down the bodice in a narrow sliver (that includes covered buttons) to the belted waist.

JEAN LOUIS

(1907–1997)

SEEMINGLY BORN INTO A FASHION CAREER IN PARIS, JEAN LOUIS BEGAN AS A TEENAGED SKETCH ARTIST FOR ESTABLISHED COUTURIERS, NONE OF WHOM INVITED HIM TO CONTRIBUTE HIS OWN DESIGNS. After immigrating to New York in 1935, he was mentored by Hattie Carnegie and sold his first design to actress Irene Dunne. With the Carnegie house he designed for the likes of the Duchess of Windsor and Gertrude Lawrence. He moved to Hollywood in 1943 and immediately established himself as the head designer for Columbia Pictures. Among many others, he dressed Lucille Ball, Rosalind Russell, Joan Crawford, Kim Novak, Doris Day, Ginger Rogers, and Loretta Young. He married Young years later, to the surprise of many, at age eighty-six.

During the mid 1940s, he labored to refine the image of Columbia's resident sex goddess, Rita Hayworth. In the process, he won movie immortality for the black strapless satin gown she wore to perform "Put the Blame on Mame" in *Gilda*. Jean Louis won an overdue Oscar in 1956 for Judy Holiday's wardrobe in *The Solid Gold Cadillac*.

In *A Hero's Life*, his 2000 biography of Joe DiMaggio, Richard Ben Cramer states that Jean Louis was creating a wedding dress for Marilyn. The final fitting was to have taken place on August 6, the day following her sudden death. Another source adds that it was a $1,600 "spangled" gown. Jean Louis never said anything for publication about this, but the idea of Marilyn wearing such a dress for a remarriage seems unlikely. In fact, the gown was being designed for her to wear in October 1962 to the Washington D.C. opening of *Mr. President*, Irving Berlin's new musical. Marilyn may have indeed been planning a wedding to DiMaggio—but definitely not in spangles.

MARILYN BY JEAN LOUIS

Gorgeous.

In April 1948, Marilyn signed a one-picture deal to costar in what she later referred to as "a nine-day wonder." When she reported to Columbia Pictures for the low budget *Ladies of the Chorus*, she was automatically given the Rita Hayworth house style in terms of hair, costuming, and even choreography for her two musical numbers.

For "Anyone Can See I Love You," she wore this gown with a heavily embellished bodice and a sheer cut-out center over a skirt of flowing chiffon. It complemented the romantic tone of the number and moved gracefully as Marilyn danced.

JEAN LOUIS

"Every Baby Needs a Da-da-daddy" was a sly song that revealed Marilyn as a budding siren in the otherwise purely sweet ingénue she played in the movie. The high-waisted evening dress of black chiffon featured a lattice pattern over the bodice and full sleeves. Vertical rows of large sequins covered the skirt. Fishnet stockings added a hint of burlesque sexiness.

Both of the dance costumes were the work of Jean Louis, though they were not specifically designed for Monroe. Like the off-stage outfits she wore in the movie, they were simply part of Columbia's stock wardrobe, left over from earlier films.

Twelve years later, Marilyn was now a superstar of the highest order, and she requested Jean Louis to design her clothes for *The Misfits*. Ironically, like *Ladies of the Chorus*, it was not to be an extensive wardrobe and included nothing as glamorous as the sparkly evening gowns she wore in their first collaboration.

In July 1960, Marilyn posed in Manhattan for these costume tests. Here she is in a slip of silver satin with a generous portion of black lace at the bust and hem. She wears the slip in the opening moments of *The Misfits*, and she would don it after completing the film for a series of sexy poses distributed to magazines, including *Playboy*.

This lovely day dress was made of ivory silk with a pattern of pale green peacock "eyes." There is a self-tie at the waist and a supporting seam under the bust that leads to soft pleating into the center of the skirt. The design is slightly reminiscent of the famous "subway" dress from *The Seven Year Itch*, with a tighter skirt. Marilyn did not end up wearing this design in the film, though she did retain the fur wrap. She liked this dress, however, and wore it to two parties held on location in Reno—a press reception to launch production, and later at a joint birthday party for Clark Gable's wife and director John Huston.

JEAN LOUIS

Rehearsing an early scene from *The Misfits*, filmed on the streets of Reno, Marilyn is in a black silk crepe cocktail dress with a scoop-necked bolero jacket and matching black pumps. She offset the black with white gloves and matching bag.

The dress without the jacket shows off the irregular neckline threaded with a jersey band. As was the industry custom, more than one copy of this dress was made, and as was *her* custom, Marilyn kept one for her personal use. A year after completing *The Misfits*, she was photographed wearing it on a date with Frank Sinatra in Las Vegas. Her copy, including the jacket, was sold at Christie's Monroe auction in 1999.

Recently, costume and fabric expert Wayne Murray acquired the version she wears in these photos, and he found the interior of it to be quite revealing. He discovered two small "falsies" sewn in just below the neckline. Marilyn, of course, had beautiful breasts but they sloped down and out a bit. This gave them a perky profile, but they weren't as fully rounded on top as she liked for certain styles, so she relied on this slight padding to fill out the neckline of the dress to her satisfaction. In fairness to Monroe, it should be noted that her use of this padding was not an attempt to appear bigger but rather to enhance the impact of the dress. She was, after all, a girl who felt secure enough in her breast size to go braless 90 percent of the time. But when it came to how her body was presented in clothes, she was an unapologetic perfectionist.

In addition to the padding, Murray found a Western Costume label. "Movies like *The Misfits*, that were made independently of major studios," Murray says, "sent their wardrobes [after filming] to these costume warehouses, where they could be rented out randomly. MGM, Fox, or Paramount would place them in their own vast costume collections, to be worn in the future only in their own productions."

Monroe makes sure her wig is fitted properly while her costars, Montgomery Clift and Clark Gable, look on. She is wearing the most famous costume from *The Misfits*. Known as "the cherry dress," it is white rayon and features self ties at the shoulder that lead to a deep "V" bodice. The wrap skirt is finished in a tulip hem.

Two years later, Jean Louis worked with Marilyn for *Something's Got to Give*. Here, on the set in the spring of 1962, Marilyn wears an appropriately spring-like design. It is a wide-spaced floral print backless dress in jersey with a subtle draping effect at the rear waist.

Louis was pleased to find Monroe several pounds lighter than she had been in *The Misfits*. She was, in fact, slimmer than she had been in years. The weight loss began a year earlier following her divorce from Arthur Miller and after gall-bladder surgery forced her onto a strict diet.

Vogue magazine noted Monroe's sleek figure and in June had her photographed for a layout that was published after her death. It was the first time she got to don authentic high fashion. She modeled Dior gowns and furs by Maximillian.

Costar Cyd Charisse joins Marilyn for a scene of catty dialogue from *Something's Got to Give*. Marilyn is in a suit of beige wool with mink at the collar, cuffs, and hemline. A matching mink beret, a slim silk clutch, silk gloves, and a diamond and platinum brooch add up to a chic totality. This lovely suit has been characterized as a Hollywood interpretation of the ubiquitous "Jackie Look" that had been setting fashion standards since the Kennedy inauguration.

   Marilyn was delighted with the costumes for *Something's Got to Give*, and she, Jean Louis, and costar Dean Martin began the project with optimism.

JEAN LOUIS

75

May 19, 1962: Marilyn Monroe arrives at Madison Square Garden in Manhattan to perform at a star-studded gala forty-fifth birthday celebration for President John Kennedy. She is escorted by her former father-in-law, Isidore Miller.

When the event's producer, Jean Dalrymple, invited Marilyn to participate, she made her promise to dress with decorum. "I told her to wear something modest," Dalrymple recalled, "because it was a formal occasion." Marilyn, of course, had blithely ignored a similar admonishment six years earlier when preparing to meet Queen Elizabeth.

To design her gown, Marilyn turned to Jean Louis. In addition to his movie work, Louis was known for the seemingly see-through costumes he engineered for Marlene Dietrich's concerts. Marilyn asked him to create something "historic" for her that would show off her newly slim figure and wow the crowd.

Berniece Miracle (Marilyn's half sister) recalled: "Jean Louis sketched two possibilities. Both were formfitting. One was covered in sequins, the other in rhinestones. One dipped to the waist in back; the other was *décolleté*.' 'Berniece, which do you think I should wear?' [asked Monroe] 'Well honey, you know which side I think is your best.'"

What Marilyn chose was more modern and less fussy than Jean Louis' designs for Dietrich. It is a clinging, floor-length sheath. Cut low in back, and sleeveless, it has a scoop neck and incorporated shoulder straps. Its unique feature is the fabric. "Nude, very thin material," Jean Louis said, "embroidered with rhinestones so she would shine in the spotlight. She wore nothing, absolutely nothing, underneath." The rhinestones were set in a graduated rosette motif, and the fit was so tight the designer included a slit of eighteen inches in the back, so Marilyn could walk. To complement the gown, she swathed herself in white mink until she began her song.

Marilyn paid Jean Louis $5,000 for the "JFK Dress." At the Christies auction of Monroe belongings in 1999, it sold for over $1,267,500.

JEAN LOUIS

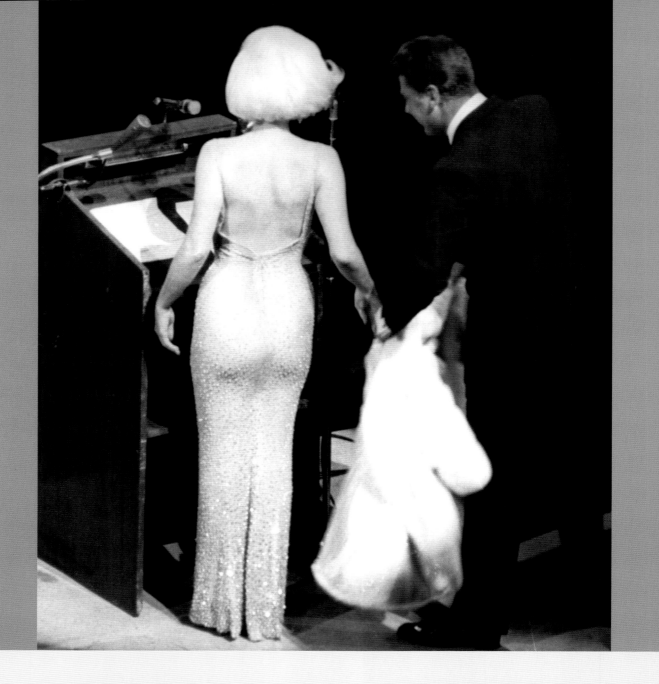

Peter Lawford tends to Marilyn's fur as she takes the stage to croon "Happy Birthday" to JFK as the last act of the evening. "There was a hush over the whole place when I came on to sing," Marilyn told *Life* magazine two months later. "Like if I had been wearing a slip I would have thought it was showing or something. I thought, 'Oh, my gosh, what if no sound comes out?!'"

The hush was the result of pure awe. The exquisite glittering vision the audience beheld flew in the face of a year of several unflattering press photos of Marilyn looking wan and unhappy. Here suddenly was America's greatest female star back in gorgeous shape and as dazzling and daring as ever. Her voice didn't fail her, and though she seems a little tipsy in the only film footage from the performance, she stole the show from Maria Callas, Jack Benny, Peggy Lee, Harry Belafonte, and Shirley MacLaine. Some critics felt Monroe's performance was inappropriately seductive in the presence of a president, but Kennedy loved it. (This was years before the general public became aware that he and Marilyn were alleged to be lovers).

This most famous performance ever of the most common song in the world became another instant Monroe landmark. It also recalled a childhood dream of Marilyn's about standing nude in front of a vast crowd. "My impulse to appear naked and my dreams about it had no shame or sin in them. Dreaming of people looking at me made me feel less lonely, I think. I wanted them to see me naked because I was ashamed of my clothes. I wore the never changing faded blue dress of poverty. Naked, I was like the other girls and not someone in an orphan's uniform." Now, with worlds separating her from her orphanage days, and just a whisper of material and four thousand rhinestones barely shielding her nakedness from the stadium crowd, the childhood dream came the closest it ever would to reality—and in front of the President of the United States no less.

Monroe continued to mesmerize at the party afterwards (seen here with celebrity promoter Earl Blackwell). Adlai Stevenson characterized her that evening as "dressed in what she called 'skin and beads.' I didn't see the beads!" Arthur Schlesinger Jr. wrote in his journal: "I do not think I have ever seen anyone so beautiful."

The simple clean lines of Marilyn's gown continued to be a popular pattern for the remainder of the 1960s. The most enduring fashion statement of this legendary evening, however, was Monroe's hairstyle.*

* See the Hair Salon section (page 220)

JEAN LOUIS

Three Jean Louis costume sketches: A slip and a bikini designed for *The Misfits*, and an illustration of the JFK birthday dress done after the fact.

On June 1, 1962 (her thirty-sixth birthday), Marilyn makes her final public appearance as she runs on the field of newly opened Chavez Ravine (later named Dodger) Stadium. She is accompanied by L.A. Angels' outfielder Albie Pearson. A capacity crowd roared a greeting as Monroe made a pre-game appeal for the Muscular Dystrophy Foundation. Just as she had so often at the start of her years at Fox, Marilyn borrowed a movie costume for this event.

JEAN LOUIS

JOHN MOORE

(1928–1996)

THIS UNSUNG HERO OF THE MARILYN MONROE FASHION STORY WAS BORN IN OKLAHOMA AND RAISED IN TEXAS. Directly after high school John Moore* moved to New York City to study fashion. He graduated from the Parsons School of Design in 1948 and immediately got work designing for Elizabeth Arden and Mattie Talmack. It was at Talmack's that he met Norman Norell, who became a mentor.

In 1953 Moore and Talmack both earned special Coty Awards for "noteworthy contributions to fashion." It was through Norell that Moore met Marilyn in 1955. Close in age, the two became instant friends. Monroe appreciated Moore's taste so much she let him have a strong hand in decorating the 57th Street apartment she shared with Arthur Miller.

In addition to Monroe, John Moore created personal wardrobe for Angela Lansbury and sultry nightclub star Lisa Kirk. His greatest moment of fame came in 1965, when Lady Bird Johnson chose him to design her inaugural gown, a flowing A-line dress in a "Yellow-Rose-of-Texas" color with a matching floor-length coat in satin with sable trimmed cuffs. Critics unfairly gave the design a hard time, mainly because they missed the incomparable style of Jacqueline Kennedy. The gown now resides in the Smithsonian Institution. Other Moore designs are in the permanent collections of several museums, including the Metropolitan Museum of Art. In the '70s, Moore fell off the fashion radar.

*Not to be confused with John Moore, a costume and production designer for such films as *El Cid*, *A Farewell to Arms*, and *The Fall of the Roman Empire*.

Marilyn poses for Cecil Beaton in an improvised studio at Manhattan's Ambassador Hotel early in 1956. Famed as a gifted portrait photographer of luminaries from the arts and high society, Beaton was also renowned for his costume designs for *My Fair Lady*, *Gigi*, and *On a Clear Day You Can See Forever*. As other photographers had, Beaton marveled at Monroe's ability to offer him an endless variety of poses and expressions. He later wrote of her, "Whatever press agentry or manufactured illusion may have lit the fuse, it is her own weird genius that has sustained her flight . . . she will never die."

For the Beaton sitting, one of her favorites, Marilyn wore several outfits, including this classic "little black dress" in velvet by John Moore. The shoelace shoulder straps hold up a sweetheart neckline.

JOHN MOORE

83

Of course Marilyn didn't wear designer duds all the time during her years in New York. Free of makeup, wearing tweed slacks, penny loafers, a favorite old polo coat, and a scarf covering her hair, she would attend classes at the Actor's Studio and explore the streets of Manhattan unrecognized and unbothered. She loved it. "I like to be really dressed up, or really undressed," Marilyn said with a wink to *Cosmopolitan*. "I don't bother with anything in between."

The same dress Marilyn wore for Cecil Beaton suffered a highly publicized wardrobe malfunction on February 3, 1956 when one of the shoulder straps gave way during a press reception being held at the Plaza Hotel. Monroe was interviewed and photographed alongside Laurence Olivier who was being announced as her costar and director for the upcoming comedy *The Prince and the Showgirl*, to be filmed in England.

When Monroe's dress strap failed, she was offered a safety pin by reporter Judith Crist, but that didn't hold. After posing for several photos, Marilyn became offended when it was suggested that the stunt had been planned. Olivier believed it had been, and for fun he created a similar moment for one of Marilyn's early scenes in their movie.

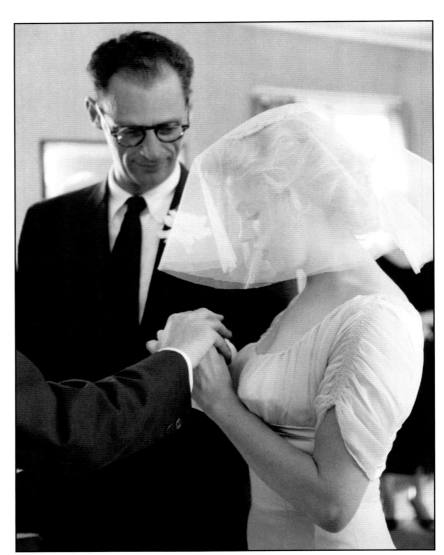

Marilyn and Arthur Miller are married on July 1, 1956 at the home of his agent, Kay Brown, in Katonah, New York. Marilyn is wearing a John Moore sheath in soft beige chiffon with ruching on the sleeves and bodice and a satin sash under the bust line. She wore matching satin pumps and her friend, Amy Greene, contributed a white "halo veil of soft lace" that was soaked in coffee to attain a matching beige shade.

Wardrobe illustration
by Michelle Shin

For the rowdy New York premiere of *The Prince and the Showgirl* at Radio City Music Hall on June 13, 1957, Marilyn chose this John Moore gown. Two weeks earlier, *Screen Parade* writer Herbert Kamm, who described himself as a married "red-blooded American male," was at Monroe's 57th Street apartment when Moore came by. "Miss Monroe's clothes designer minced into the room," Kamm wrote, "with samples of material for the gown she would wear to the opening of her film. His feather-cut sandy hair was combed forward, and he spoke in a velvety voice."

His homophobia aside, Kamm's article tells us that Moore brought satin swatches in burgundy, "embossed Kelly green," turquoise, and the champagne beige that had accented her wedding dress. "Oh golly," Marilyn enthused, "they're all so lovely."

The burgundy was dismissed as a "dowager's color," the green as too typical for a movie star. Kamm pushed for the turquoise, but wisely, Marilyn chose the beige. "I rather like this," she said. "Maybe I'm a little sentimental about it."

With its skin-tight fit, fishtail skirt, and long matching stole, the dress could have easily overwhelmed even Marilyn Monroe had it been made in anything more vivid than beige. Knowing the gown was enough of a glamour statement on its own, Marilyn wore an unstructured hairstyle and a natural makeup palette.

JOHN MOORE

This is one of the few designs
Monroe wore that brings to
mind "bullet bra," or worse,
"torpedo tits." She almost
always preferred a more
natural look. She liked John
Moore's designs though
because he constructed
the bust lines in his gowns
so that they lifted Marilyn's
breasts without undergarments.
In this instance, they give
the illusion that she was more
endowed than she really was.

Her exact measurements
quite naturally fluctuated
depending on her weight
and if she was going through
one of her unsuccessful
pregnancies. When slim, her
measurements were said
to be 36D-23-35, but there
were also column items that
stated she was (at one time)
38-25-36. In terms of what
are considered vintage dress
sizes, however, she would
be wearing sizes six to eight,
depending on her weight.

John Moore utilized the champagne satin once again six months later for this elegant evening suit that Marilyn wore in a fashion show to benefit the March of Dimes on January 28, 1958. The four-button jacket features a rolled collar and bracelet-length sleeves. A knee-length slit helped Monroe navigate the tight floor-length skirt.

Fashion innovator Cristobal Balenciaga introduced the formless "sack" dress in 1957. A year later he produced a more fitted version and dubbed it a "chemise." Here Marilyn wears a John Moore design that combines qualities of both. It is a boat neck style in beige knit topped by a cream-colored stand-up collar. Posing with Monroe in New York in April 1958 is producer Walter Mirisch. He and his star were announcing the upcoming production of *Some Like It Hot*.

The sack craze was short-lived. When Marilyn tired of this dress, she sent it to Berniece Miracle, who decided to have the dress reshaped into a traditional style, with imperfect results.

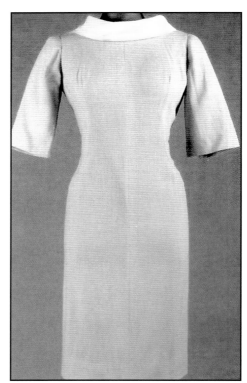

Marilyn models another
Moore chemise. This one
is in black silk and trimmed
with a rather absurd white
organza bow. Now that
Monroe's curves were
admired in every corner
of the world, she didn't
feel the need to keep
them on constant display.
By this time, she opted
for comfort over skin-tight
whenever she could.
"A sack allows you to move,"
Marilyn said. "And it moves
with you. And movement
is—well, movement is good."
Monroe also liked the
sack because she had been
putting on weight, and
it was less obvious in this
forgiving style.

JOHN MOORE

On July 7, 1958, Marilyn attends the Hollywood premiere of *Gigi* at the Paramount (now the El Capitan) Theatre. She is wearing a snug fishtail gown in red lace. Spaghetti straps support a deep neckline. Black opera-length gloves and an organza wrap contribute to the appropriate *ooh-la-la* effect.

MARILYN in FASHION

During a break in filming *Some Like It Hot* at the Hotel del Coronado in San Diego, Monroe enjoys a hearty laugh in a beige silk shift designed for comfort. Clearly John Moore loved to see Marilyn in various tones of beige. During her starlet phase, she would have considered it dull. Now, however, she shared Moore's enthusiasm for the color.

JOHN MOORE

March 28, 1959: A Rubenesque Monroe is greeted at the New York premiere of *Some Like It Hot*. Her ankle-length gown consists of ivory crepe embroidered with silver bugle beads. The halter top with shoestring straps is a style John Moore used for several of Marilyn's gowns. The skirt is worked with pendant bugle beads that added swinging movement in a sly nod to the flapper era in which *Some Like It Hot* is set. White fur, long gloves, and five-inch earrings top off the image of high glamour. The dress was also back bearing, and because Marilyn hated panty lines she wore a stripper's g-string underneath.

This gown, and one Moore made in black, became two of Marilyn's favorites. She would wear this one in her next movie *Let's Make Love*, to perform "Specialization." She is seen in the black version in Philippe Halsman's famous 1959 photo series of celebrities leaping in the air.

The Monroe figure had filled out steadily over the past two years. Several columnists suggested Marilyn invest in a good girdle. She brushed off the snipes: "You want your audience to be able to distinguish me from Tony and Jack [Curtis and Lemon, her costars in the film]. Besides, my husband likes me plump."

Montgomery Clift escorts Marilyn to the New York preview of *The Misfits* at the Capitol Theatre on January 31, 1961. The dress is black silk jersey with a black fox flourish on the hem. Marilyn wears it with a matching stole and black kid gloves.

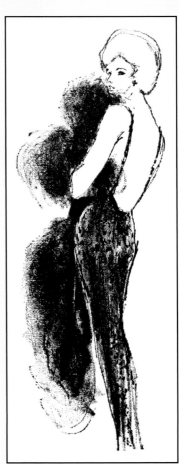

JOHN MOORE

fashion. fashion. fashion.

Marilyn is guided into Manhattan's Roseland ballroom for a gala to benefit the Actor's Studio in March 1961. She was in the midst of an exceptionally stressful period. Clark Gable, her costar in *The Misfits*, had died suddenly. Her marriage to Arthur Miller had ended bitterly and she had recently survived a brief but harrowing stay in a psychiatric hospital. Still, she had promised Lee Strasberg—her acting guru and father substitute—she would appear at this fundraiser, and although she felt emotionally battered by recent events, she kept her word. Her look for the evening was one of subdued elegance. Under the fur (clutched like a security blanket), is the black version of the John Moore design she wore at the *Some Like It Hot* premiere. By this time, Marilyn had narrowed her color palette down to four choices for such high profile public occasions: beige, black, white, and flesh-colored/see-through.

May 13, 1959: Monroe is photographed for the first time in a John Moore cocktail dress that would be her go-to outfit for the next three years. She is accepting an award at the Italian embassy in Manhattan for her performance in *The Prince and the Showgirl* from the David di Donatello Italian film society. With her is Anna Magnani, a winner for *Wild Is the Wind*.

JOHN MOORE

This short, sleeveless dress of black wool crepe had a matching cropped jacket. The bodice was made of coffee-colored chiffon embroidered with black scrolling foliage dotted with tiny beads. Marilyn wore the dress to meet Russian premiere Nikita Khrushchev when he visited Hollywood in September of 1959. She wore it to the christening of Clark Gable's son in January 1961, and later in the year she was seen in the dress as she sat ringside with Dean Martin to hear Frank Sinatra sing in Las Vegas. In February 1962, she was photographed in it while being serenaded by a mariachi band in Mexico City.

Here Marilyn wears the dress while chatting with Gene Kelly and Yves Montand on the set of *Let's Make Love*. Marilyn can be seen in the dress in the film's sexy final scene.

Two years later she is in the dress again for hairstyle tests on the set of *Something's Got to Give*—most likely the last time she donned this favored John Moore design.

JOHN MOORE

99

NORMAN NORELL

(1900–1972)

DESPITE WONDERFUL REACTION TO HER PERFORMANCE IN *THE SEVEN YEAR ITCH*, TWENTIETH CENTURY-FOX PRESSURED MARILYN TO APPEAR IN FILMS SHE FELT WERE UNWORTHY AND REFUSED TO GIVE HER A LONG OVERDUE SALARY INCREASE. Late in 1954, she walked defiantly out on her contract and retreated to Manhattan, where she enrolled in the esteemed Actor's Studio under the tutelage of Lee Strasberg.

On suspension from the studio, Marilyn joined forces with the brilliant photographer Milton Greene to form her own production company. She grew close to Greene's elegant wife, Amy, a former model who would become Monroe's most influential fashion advisor. The seventy garments Marilyn brought with her from storage in Los Angeles, which included the Ceil Chapman dress she wore on stage in Korea and a beige Don Loper suit, failed to impress Amy Greene. "It dawned on me what pitiful clothes she had," she told Monroe biographer Anthony Summers. "She had to rummage through my drawers every time we wanted to go out. We brought Norman Norell to dinner . . . and had him design an elegant wardrobe for her."

Recipient in 1943 of the first Coty Fashion Award ever presented, Indiana-born Norman Norell studied at Brooklyn's Pratt Institute before designing costumes for such stars as Rudolph Valentino and Gloria Swanson in the early '20s for the Famous Players Astoria film studio in Queens.

In 1928 Norell became head designer for style icon Hattie Carnegie and then in 1941 established his own line. By the time he met Marilyn Monroe he was considered one of the premiere designers in the country—the equal of any of Europe's top names. His specialties included "evening shirtwaists, sequined 'mermaid dresses,' sailor-inspired clothing . . . and simple wool dresses with high necklines." He also worked in a fabric called "slipper satin." Norell was the perfect choice to refine Monroe's image and ease her entry into the *beau monde* that was Manhattan in the mid-'50s.

MARILYN BY NORELL

On January 7, 1955, Marilyn unveils her first Norell as she holds a press conference in a Manhattan town house to announce the formation of Marilyn Monroe Productions. This is a silvery satin sheath with spaghetti straps. A pair of white stockings (which had to be acquired at a nurses' uniform shop), white pumps, white opera-length gloves, and a luxurious white ribbed ermine coat lined in black silk from Maximillian, added to the sleek effect. Dangling diamond-and-pearl earrings were borrowed from Van Cleef & Arpels, and Marilyn admitted they were the first real diamonds she had ever worn.

In March 1955, at the opening of the play *Cat on a Hot Tin Roof* on Broadway, Marilyn shimmers in this coppery toned lamé gown that fit like a second skin.

Joe DiMaggio accompanies a radiant Marilyn to a June 1, 1955 screening of *The Seven Year Itch* in Manhattan. The cocktail dress is in white satin. As usual, Monroe has pulled the straps off her shoulders. She complemented the dress with a white mink stole, short white gloves, a white silk clutch, and newly-invented white spring-o-lators from Herbert Levine shoes.

NORMAN NORELL

Monroe is encased in one of Norell's signature "mermaid" evening gowns as she and Arthur Miller enter a party at the Waldorf Astoria hotel following the premiere of *Baby Doll,* in December 1956. This gown, with its halter-style top, plunging neckline, and bare back is in navy blue jersey, heavily embroidered in matching blue sequins. Several months later she wore the gown for a return to the Waldorf for an "April in Paris" party thrown by Elsa Maxwell. Also in attendance were Senator John Kennedy and his wife, Jacqueline.

Wardrobe Illustration
by George Zeno

Monroe chose the Norell mermaid gown again for one of the most daringly sensual poses of her career, for legendary photographer Richard Avedon.

Norell design of Marilyn's life was one she wore to the January 1962 Golden Globe Awards at th
tel. She was being honored as the "World's Favorite" female star. It was the first high-profile
ded in Hollywood in four years, and she wanted to make a dazzling impression. The deep emer
r-length evening gown is covered in matching sequins with an inset waistband. Marilyn carrie
and wore emerald-and-diamond earrings, a gift from Frank Sinatra.

dd configuration of the armholes and neckline of this dress has been a subject of conjecture
. Did Monroe mistakenly wear the dress backwards? Did she not realize her arms were suppo
ie slots on either side of her chest? Since the gown was back baring, it's obvious that no wom
it backwards.

N IN FASHION

Photographed for a museum showing many years later, the dress appears in the configuration Norell intended.

Because she had lost weight, Marilyn's bust had lost a bit of its voluptuousness. She worried that if she wore the dress as designed, the bodice might flatten her. She loved the dress otherwise, so she had a dressmaker add a small strap behind her neck to hold up the front of the dress, which left it looser, creating a slight "V" neckline. If Norell had a reaction to Monroe's doctoring of this design, it was never officially recorded.

NORMAN NORELL

ORRY-KELLY

(1897–1964)

IN THE 1920s, AFTER WORKING AS A WINDOW DRESSER IN SYDNEY, AUSTRALIAN ORRY-KELLY CAME TO MANHATTAN WITH ACTING ASPIRATIONS. Instead of acting, he became an illustrator for silent movies before moving into designing sets and costumes for Broadway shows. Making the move to Hollywood in 1932, he began one of the longest and most successful careers ever in costume design. At Warner Bros. he designed for *42nd Street*, *The Maltese Falcon*, and *Casablanca*. He became indispensable to Bette Davis, who worked closely with him to visually define some of her most famous characterizations. Orry-Kelly won Oscars for his work on *An American in Paris*, *Les Girls*, and *Some Like It Hot*.

Marilyn tries to avoid a blast of steam as she makes her entrance into *Some Like It Hot*. She is wearing a snug-fitting black wool traveling coat held closed by three covered buttons on her left hip. The neckline and hem are trimmed generously in monkey fur. A cloche hat in black felt boasts a cluster of egret feathers.

ORRY-KELLY

During a break in filming in the fall of 1958, Orry-Kelly makes an adjustment to the most revealing movie costume of Marilyn Monroe's career.

ORRY-KELLY
111

The famed dress is made (in Kelly's words), "of nude soufflé draped on the bias to lift her breasts and push her tummy in. It was so slightly beaded over her breasts that her nipples were not covered and [director] Billy Wilder had to light her with a single spot that left the area strategically in darkness."

The skirt is covered in silver sequins of various sizes and crystal beads—some hanging below the hemline. Orry-Kelly added a small red bleeding heart appliqué to the fabric hugging Marilyn's behind. It gives the impression of a tattoo on a dress! This little flourish is not visible in the film. Perhaps it was a twist on the old adage of wearing one's heart on one's sleeve. If it was a private joke between designer and star, its meaning has been lost to posterity—or posterior as the case may be.

Marilyn wore the costume for a seduction scene with Tony Curtis and to croon a lusty version of "I Want To Be Loved By You." Moviegoers, mesmerized by the sensuous swaying of her close-to-nude breasts during the song, had a surprise coming. When she finished the number and turned her back to the camera, the dress turned out to be backless–down to M. M.'s tailbone. The effect elicited gasps from audiences. Today, of course, more revealing costumes are seen frequently on *Dancing with the Stars*, but at the time only a handful of European actresses showed more skin on film.

For Marilyn's final scenes in the film, Orry-Kelly placed her in the same nude soufflé, this time with black sequins and bead work and a more plunging neckline. He also added black bead appliqués of butterfly shapes on the skirt, and one sitting atop Marilyn's right shoulder. Two years later, this costume ended up on Barbara Nichols for her performance as famed nightclub queen Texas Guinan in *The George Raft Story*.

EMILIO PUCCI

(1914–1992)

IN ADDITION TO HIS INNOVATIVE, AWARD-WINNING CAREER IN FASHION, EMILIO PUCCI WAS A MAN OF REMARKABLE ACCOMPLISHMENTS. Born into Florentine nobility, he was an avid sportsman who excelled at swimming, fencing, tennis, and car racing. His skiing prowess earned him a scholarship and a chance to accompany the Italian ski team to the 1932 Olympics in Lake Placid. He earned degrees in social science in Italy, political science in Oregon, and studied agriculture in Georgia. During World War II, he served in the Italian Air Force as a torpedo bomber, and supported Italy's fascist regime. He helped Benito Mussolini's eldest daughter, a personal friend, escape Italy after the collapse of her father's reign.

His first designs were for his ski team in 1947. A fashion reporter spotted them on the slopes, and he encouraged Pucci to design some additional pieces for a *Harper's Bazaar* layout. He did, and his design career was launched. Soon, he not only designed but also oversaw the invention of new fabrics. "Pucci makes full use of the textile technology of the times," *Vogue* wrote of his innovations.

When he designed a collection of scarves in bold colors and prints he was advised to try the graphics on blouses and dresses. They were an immediate hit, and he was soon being called the Prince of Prints. In addition to Marilyn, he was also favored by Audrey Hepburn, Gina Lollobrigida, Sophia Loren, and, in the 1980s, by Madonna. The Pucci name remains relevant today. Jennifer Lopez caused a sensation in a skin-tight Pucci with revealing cut outs at a gala welcoming the Duke and Duchess of Cambridge to Los Angeles in July 2011.

MARILYN BY PUCCI

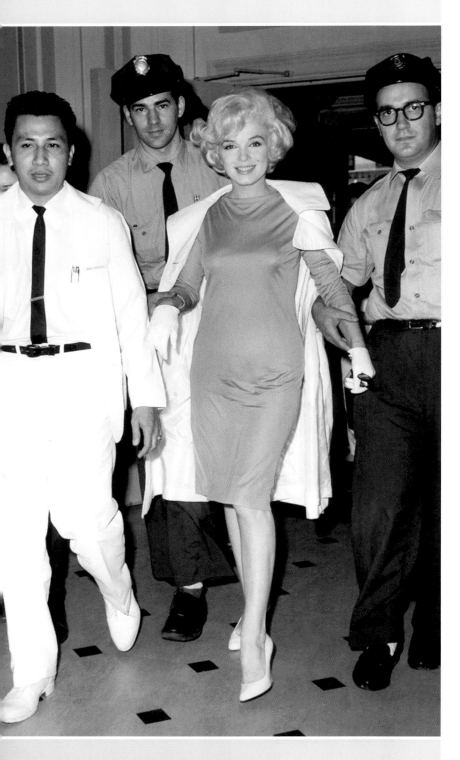

Marilyn faces a mob as she is escorted from a Manhattan hospital on July 11, 1961 following gallbladder surgery. She is in a Pucci sheath of either tan or green. The lines of the dress—one of several in her wardrobe—herald the look of the new decade. It is knee-length with a boat neckline and long sleeves—which Monroe always pushed up. At the time, the dress caused fewer comments than did her new sculpted hairstyle by Kenneth Battelle.

Marilyn discovered the Pucci line a couple of months earlier while shopping on Fifth Avenue. Susan Strasberg, Lee's actress daughter, told a story about being with her when she first saw a similar Pucci sheath. With no false modesty she said, "Gee, if it fits the hanger that well, imagine what it could look like on me!" Marilyn was attracted to the "wrinkle-free silk that clung" Pucci had developed and utilized to create blouses and shifts that combined simple lines with vibrant colors and prints.

Going out shopping with a girlfriend was something Monroe had seldom done, and she found she enjoyed it. In a 1972 piece for *MS* magazine, Gloria Steinem found this quote from 1961: "Another new thing is shopping. I was never much interested in clothes, except for public appearances . . . but the other day . . . I bought a pale yellow sweater. I never wear yellow, but now I will. And, I never used to wear blue, but I do now . . . I've found out it's fun to go shopping. It's such a feminine thing to do."

Marilyn is photographed at a press conference in Mexico City in February 1962. She is wearing a mint green Pucci shift.

Monroe is photographed visiting an orphanage in Mexico City. She was in the Mexican capitol primarily to shop for furnishings for her new Spanish-style home in Brentwood. She is in a Pucci print in vivid shades of green, yellow, and pink. This time, she is also wearing the self-belt that came with all of the designer's sheaths. She often carried a solid-colored nylon scarf with these dresses for a subtle touch of glamour and also to cling to when facing the ever-present crew of reporters and photographers.

In July, 1962, just weeks before her death, Marilyn posed for photographer and friend George Barris in what would be her final full photo session. She was captured in an orange bikini at the Santa Monica Beach and here at a borrowed home in the hills above the Sunset Strip. She is in a Pucci print blouse in pumpkin, gold, and cream, worn over snug capri pants in pumpkin by Jax. The look was informal, sexy, stylish, and *very* California. It was exactly what Marilyn wanted after her final bruising year in New York.

The print, with its Italianate graphics, may not seem like typical Pucci. Instead, it resembles similar designs by Gianni Versace that appeared twenty years later.

In a 1995 book about this session, George Barris recalled that Marilyn sent him to Beverly Hills to buy the wardrobe for their shoot. "At Jax he bought her some beautiful slacks and decorative Emilio Pucci sport shirts. Then off to Saks [Fifth Avenue] for a bulky sweater, terry-cloth three-quarter hooded beach jacket, a blanket, a large towel, and a sexy bikini." Barris did indeed buy the beach paraphernalia, and it's possible (though not likely) he picked up her slacks, but Monroe brought everything else.

She wore the blouse a year earlier when she visited Joe DiMaggio in Florida, and the orange bikini was a Pucci she bought in New York. The "bulky sweater" was not something Saks Fifth Avenue would have carried at the time.*

*For the story behind the sweater Marilyn wore in the Barris layout, see the Sweater Girl (page 272).

"I like to feel blonde all over."

When Christies in New York staged their auction of Monroe effects in 1999, they put up this display of her Pucci wardrobe, including (on the far right) the blouse she wears in the prior photograph.

There is speculation (most likely false) that at some point Pucci and Monroe struck a mutually beneficial agreement: She would wear his designs in public, and in exchange he would supply her with clothes *gratis* or at a sizeable discount. Such deals are, of course, commonplace today. For the last year and a half of her life, Marilyn was seldom seen in anything *but* Pucci except for appearances that demanded high glamour. Even when she was laid to rest in August 1962 she was wearing a mint green Pucci shift.

Wardrobe Illustration by George Zeno

EMILIO PUCCI

RENIÉ

(aka Renié Conley, 1901–1992)

LIKE ORRY-KELLY, WASHINGTON-BORN RENIÉ BEGAN HER CAREER AS A SET DESIGNER FOR THE THEATER BEFORE TURNING TO FASHION ILLUSTRATION. By the late 1930s she was ensconced at RKO, where she designed costumes for Ginger Rogers, Lucille Ball, Lupe Vélez, and many others during her dozen years at the studio. In 1950 she joined Twentieth Century Fox. During her thirty-year career she worked on over 175 movies, ranging from *Snow White* and *The Three Stooges* to *Cleopatra*, for which she shared an Oscar with Irene Sharaff.

Renié costumed three 1951 comedies in which Marilyn Monroe served primarily as window dressing, but which nonetheless contributed to her rapid rise to stardom.

MARILYN BY RENIÉ

Renié's flattering cocktail dress is in black satin with a chiffon insert over the chest, topped with a choker-like jeweled collar. In this scene from *As Young as You Feel* with costar Wally Brown, Marilyn carried a heavily sequined black chiffon wrap. Directly from the set Marilyn wore this dress, sans the wrap and with a change of gloves, to a party on the Fox lot for a group of visiting exhibitors and columnists.

Loves it.

This offbeat design would only have been appropriate in a Hollywood version of an office environment circa 1951. It is in white wool with a deep "U" shaped neckline and an unusual shoulder treatment—giving the provocative illusion that the front and rear panels of the dress are fastened together with only two rhinestone pins.

For *As Young as You Feel*, Monroe's first film under her new Fox contract, she wears this Renié day dress of white eyelet and lace that features an interesting architectural neckline. Two earring-sized rhinestone pins sit below Marilyn's left shoulder. The dress turned up a year and a half later in another Monroe film, but not on Marilyn; Jean Peters wears it in *Niagara*.

RENIÉ

"Naturally," wrote Maurice Zolotow in his 1960 Monroe biography, "the main attraction was such stars as Anne Baxter, Dan Dailey, June Haver, Richard Widmark, and Tyrone Power. But when Marilyn arrived, an hour and a half late, it was she who was mobbed by the theatre operators and film salesmen. The exhibitors kept asking her, 'And what pictures are you going to be in, Miss Monroe?' She fluttered her eyelashes, and said, 'You'll have to ask Mr. Zanuck or Mr. Schreiber [Zanuck's first assistant] about that," Soon Spyros Skouras, the president of Twentieth Century Fox, became aware that his leading stars were being trampled to death in the stampede for Marilyn."

In *Love Nest*, Marilyn played Roberta, a former WAC and war buddy of the lead, Bill Lundigan. Though blonde and beautiful, Roberta was neither dizzy or a mantrap, thus Renié produced a more sophisticated wardrobe for the character.

For her entrance into *Love Nest*, Monroe wore this traveling suit of gray houndstooth check. Prominent turned-back cuffs match a rolled plunging collar in white. The jacket also includes three black buttons and patch pockets. A black-and-white theme is carried out in two-toned, low-heeled

Corrie was here!...
just kidding.

Marilyn is majestic in this unusual
Renié design. Originally worn by
Nina Vale—with much less impact—
in the 1945 Dick Powell movie
Cornered. The gown is made of
French Chantilly lace, a fabric used
for Victorian shawls.

Of the five films Marilyn made in 1952, *Clash By Night* offered her the least colorful character to play. On loan from Fox, she was an uncomplicated young girl in love with a fellow cannery worker in a drab fishing port. Her wardrobe was consistent with the role; there was nothing flashy about it. Here, however, Renié placed her in this spider web of a dress for portraits of high glamour. The delicate lace is stretched—as if sprayed on—over an off-white undergarment that could be either a dress or a night-gown. The high neck and long sleeves are balanced by the sexy see-through effect. Marilyn's only accessory is a pair of diamond earrings.

For a brief sunbathing scene Renié designed this cream seersucker bikini covered in hot pink polka dots. Interesting details are the double spaghetti straps, the little tie under the bosom, and the overskirt trimmed in a solid cream ruffle which matches narrower trim on top.

The bikini bathing suit, designed and named by Louis Réard and Jacques Heim, was unveiled in Paris in 1946. Five years later, the briefest bikinis were still considered too daring for on-screen wear. Marilyn wore much more revealing versions in some of her pinup photos, but here she was allowed only this ladylike suit that barely qualifies to be called a bikini. Still, her appearance in the suit on the set caused a mob of gawking studio employees to swarm the soundstage until finally director Joseph M. Newman ordered the set closed to all but essential personnel.

For a photo layout taken during the production of *Let's Make it Legal*, but unrelated to it, Renié designed this showy one-piece swimsuit that places black lace over a metallic latex fabric. Marilyn, always conscious of how every feature of her body would photograph, is on tiptoe to give her legs an impression of more length. This was a trick she apparently learned even before she began modeling. In a family photo taken on the beach with Berniece Miracle, Norma Jeane is standing on her toes. Seen with Marilyn are actors Nick Savani and Craig Hill (on diving board), restauranteur Herman Hover (holding plant), and actress Mala Powers.

Though the character of Roberta was an army veteran, she had to be ultra feminine for a jealous-wife angle of the *Love Nest* screenplay to work. To that end, Renié created this black chiffon peignoir. It is trimmed luxuriously in Spanish lace detail down the center, on each shoulder, and in a graceful train. Marilyn wears it over a bias-cut satin slip dress with front lace detailing.

NEWMAN A635-
MARILYN MONROE
AS "ROBERTA"
CH #8
INT. APT. DOORWAY
133

4/5/51   DES RENIE

Monroe wears this cocktail dress for a party scene that closes *Love Nest*. It is in black crepe. A chiffon insert over the bust line is held up by self-ties at the shoulders. (With its short hip flounce of black chiffon and its bombshell profile, this dress could have come directly from the design house of Ceil Chapman). Ankle strap sandals are a sexy finishing touch.

Marilyn liked this and all of the designs Renié did for her over the course of their three movies. Moreover, she found the designer warm and sensitive. In appreciation she signed a copy of this photograph: "To Renié—Someone with 'feeling.' I'm more grateful than words can express. Love & thanks, Marilyn."

In *Let's Make It Legal*, Marilyn played a golddigger in this delectable Renié design made of nude crepe covered in off-white lace in a stylized floral-and-leaf pattern. The sides of the bustline fold over into an off-the-shoulder sleeve. Marilyn posed for publicity photos in the dress alongside fellow starlet Barbara Bates. Both girls had impressed

Marilyn's penchant for wearing her costumes away from the studio began here, when she chose this dress for a press party she attended with her friend and champion, columnist Sydney Skolsky.

WILLIAM TRAVILLA

(1920–1990)

LIKE MARILYN, TRAVILLA WAS BORN IN LOS ANGELES. A child prodigy, he was allowed to take adult classes at the prestigious Chouinard Art Institute when he was only eight. As a teen he began designing costumes for local burlesque stars, after admiring their photos outside theaters in downtown Los Angeles. His first job was with the Western Costume company "where he began ghost-sketching drawings for studio designers," writes his biographer, Andrew Hansford. Through another costume company he got work creating clothes for ice-skating star and actress Sonja Henie.

He began his studio career with one movie on the Hal Roach lot in 1941. For nine years after that at Columbia and Warner Bros., he dressed everyone from Shirley Temple to Lupe Vélez before joining Twentieth Century Fox. He shared a 1950 Academy Award with Leah Rhodes and Marjorie Best for *The Adventures of Don Juan*, and he created costumes for *The Day the Earth Stood Still*. By the time he was introduced to Marilyn in late 1951 he had worked on thirty-five films.

For the next five years Travilla created some of the most recognizable movie costumes of all time for Marilyn Monroe. She became his muse and even for a brief time, his lover. "Marilyn has the most fantastically perfect figure in the world," he told *Screen Life* in 1954. "No matter how you dress her, she looks sexy." Most important to Marilyn, Travilla didn't automatically discard her suggestions. He respected her sense of what designs worked best for her movie characters, but which also enhanced her increasingly famous public image.

MARILYN BY TRAVILLA

In the fall of 1952, William Travilla adjusts a costume for *Gentlemen Prefer Blondes*. This stylish lounging outfit features a top with a crossover neckline, long sleeves in forest green jersey, a waist sash of pale lavender silk and pants in deep purple velvet. Accessories are a jet choker, matching earrings, and black sandals.

This *Monkey Business* costume is in grayish green light wool. It has covered buttons that trail from the V neckline down the skirt front. It includes a self-belt and a detail of mini pom-poms at the sleeves and on a short panel that wraps from behind.

Travilla's initial collaboration with Marilyn was on her first dramatic film, *Don't Bother to Knock*. She wore only two costumes in the movie, a mousy little day dress and this slinky nightgown. It is a chiffon peignoir in brown with a lace inset at the waist. Worn under it is a soft pink satin slip.

On *Monkey Business*, Travilla learned that Monroe wasn't fond of full skirts, regardless of how tremendously fashionable they were. For this movie, however, she had no choice. As a dizzy secretary, she shows absent-minded inventor Cary Grant how well his new formula for nylons is holding up.

Later in the film, Monroe and Grant take a tumble and end up on the floor of a roller skating rink. The full skirt was essential for the action of the scene. Before the camera rolled, Travilla laughed when he noticed Marilyn reach behind and stuff some of the skirt material between her buttocks, attempting a tighter fit.

   The dress of soft tan and beige features a modified empire-style line that leads to a full circle skirt in pleats. A self-belt keeps the skirt from billowing too much. At the neck was an interesting detail that resembled a flattened tube in beige, lined in chocolate brown. Two large gold-toned safety pins held it in place. It was in this dress that Marilyn was first photographed with her future husband, Joe DiMaggio, when he visited the *Monkey Business* set.

WILLIAM TRAVILLA

Monroe marches into pop culture history as she makes a spectacular entrance at the Miss America pageant in Atlantic City in September 1952. She had just come from serving as Grand Marshall in the pageant's parade.

Fox approved her participation in the day's events, but would never have sanctioned this ankle-length Travilla dress. Made of clinging navy jersey, the design includes a plunging neckline that ends at a self-belt. Two short wings move off the hips from beneath the belt, and a front slit is knee length. A narrow white collar spreads across the shoulders and keeps the design from resembling lounging pajamas. The dress had been worn by Marilyn only for studio portraits.* It had been judged too racy for her to wear in public. Fox had selected a perfect day dress for the Atlantic City trip and Marilyn did indeed wear it to visit a children's hospital.

For the parade, however, with three thousand miles between her and the studio's control, Marilyn wore what she knew would get the most attention. Despite some criticism that she up-staged the pageant contestants, Marilyn won over the public with the sly wit she was becoming known for: "I wasn't aware of any objectionable décolletage on my part. I'd noticed people looking at me all day, but I thought they were looking at my Grand Marshall's badge."

When Hugh Hefner published his first issue of *Playboy* magazine in December 1953, he ran a centerfold of Marilyn's nude calendar pose and placed a picture of her in this Atlantic City dress on the cover. Hefner would later say that by admitting she had posed nude for the calendar shots (and that she was not ashamed), she had fired one of the first salvos in the sexual revolution. With the publication of *Playboy* Hefner had, of course, done the same.

*Marilyn was wearing this dress when she sat for the headshot later used by Andy Warhol as the basis for his iconic portrait of her.

THIS IS
EVERYTHING

Finally, with *Gentlemen Prefer Blondes*, Bill Travilla got the chance to costume Marilyn in high glamour. For the film's opening number, "Two Little Girls from Little Rock," he dressed her and costar Jane Russell in these spectacular gowns with matching feathered headpieces. They are in heavy silk crepe with thousands of sequins spiraling in every direction. The sequins start small near the top of the dress, and then enlarge as they move down—the largest being at the hem. On the left sleeve, Travilla inserted silver and white sequins, giving the impression of built-in bracelets. A diamond brooch anchors a deep slit that starts above the thigh. Sheer body-toned fabric around the neck to the waist gives the impression of bare skin. Travilla finished the look with open-toed pumps and red tinted stockings. This costume of Marilyn's brought $1.2 million at the auction of Debbie Reynolds' movie memorabilia in June 2011.

GODDESS.

Marilyn is as scrumptious as sherbet in this Travilla design. It is a body conscious ruched chiffon gown to just below the knee, where a graceful skirt then flows to the ground. It is trimmed with crystal beading. Marilyn wears it for this eye-popping entrance she and her *Blondes* costar Jane Russell make into a cruise-ship dining room. The color choice was a bold one. Many women avoid orange as it doesn't flatter all skin tones. On Marilyn, who loved the color, it managed to enhance her complexion rather than overpower it.

Marilyn poses at the Hollywood Bowl with the Ames Brothers during a benefit performance in July 1953. She is wearing especially heavy makeup—the better to be seen by the audience in the cavernous venue.

WILLIAM TRAVILLA

Glamour was one thing, but Travilla went way out on a limb with this proposed costume for Monroe's big solo number, "Diamonds Are a Girl's Best Friend." It is built on a fishnet body stocking, and smothered in rhinestones and crystals of every size and shape. Some have been clustered in bands around her hips and others drape her shoulders and breasts. Still others hang from her neckline and crotch. Her long black gloves are adorned with still more glass, as is her neck. Black ostrich feathers serve as redundant accessories. "It's like a black silk stocking all over," Marilyn told a reporter, "and just as clingy and has jewels dangling from it in all the right places."

Exposing plenty of skin, especially below the waist, this costume would have been right at home on a Follies Bergère showgirl. Which is exactly what Travilla had in mind as the "Diamonds" number was to take place in a Parisian nightclub. It's difficult to imagine, however, how Monroe would have gracefully maneuvered the song's dance steps in this creation without looking awkward or worse, vulgar—or both.

Fox executives took one look at this costume and howled in protest. Marilyn had recently survived the scandal of her 1949 nude photos appearing on a widely distributed calendar. They were in no mood to fan the flames: Put her in something "absolutely sexless" they demanded. The result was the legendary moment captured on film seen in the photo to the left.

WILLIAM TRAVILLA

As Lorelei Lee, Marilyn poses on the set of *Gentlemen Prefer Blondes*. She is in the midst of filming "Diamonds Are a Girl's Best Friend." She is costumed in Travilla's second design for the song. It is a floor-length strapless gown belted at the waist in hot pink. Its one embellishment is a large bow tied at the back, lined in black velvet. To stand up to the rigors of the song's choreography the gown was made of satin upholstery fabric, lined with felt for added stiffness. "On Monroe, it moved sensuously anyway," Travilla said.

The dress is accessorized with matching pink opera-length gloves that were placed high on her arms to create a continuous straight line extending from neckline. Flashy rhinestone bracelets and an elaborate rhinestone choker brought lots of sparkle. Marilyn's open-toed pumps are barely visible in the film.

In 1985, Madonna paid homage to "Diamond's Are a Girl's Best Friend" in her "Material Girl" video.

WILLIAM TRAVILLA

Monroe is breathtaking at the Hollywood premiere of *Call Me Madam* on March 25, 1953. She is in a sleek white satin strapless column dress, belted at the waist. The design is very similar to the pink costume in which she sang "Diamonds Are a Girl's Best Friend," except this is more form fitting and has no bow in the back. Marilyn wears white satin elbow-length gloves, white satin pumps, and carries a lush white fox stole. No distracting jewelry was needed.

Mermaid.

Marilyn wears the dress to receive an award from
Photoplay magazine in March 1953 at the Bever[ly]
Hills Hotel. She is named "Fastest Rising Star o[f]
1952," and as has happened in the past, he[r]
choice of attire overshadows the event.

Marilyn and costar Charles Coburn film a scene
for *Gentlemen Prefer Blondes*. In the film, Marilyn
is seen only from the rear in this brief scene. The
gown is well known to Monroe fans as she wore it
in a stunning series of color portraits that are
some of her most famous. It is in knife-pleated
gold lamé, with a halter neckline and style lines
that are somewhat Egyptian. The entire gown was
made from "one complete circle of fabric."

WILLIAM TRAVILLA

153

By twenty-first century standards, the dress seems tame (especially since the neckline had been altered upwards several inches for this event), but it was so tight Monroe had to be sewn into it. That combined with her sexy walk, created pandemonium at the award presentation. "When she wiggled through the audience to come to the podium," wrote columnist James Bacon, "her derriere looked like two puppies fighting under a silk sheet."

Another star in attendance was not amused. Joan Crawford gave an interview the next day that took Marilyn to task. "She should be told that the public likes provocative feminine personalities," she scolded, "but it also likes to know that underneath it all, the actresses are ladies."

Hollywood old-timers, who recalled Crawford's early days as an ambitious, scantily dressed flapper, snickered at her hypocrisy. In the press Marilyn responded defensively to Crawford's comments, but privately she felt chastised, and decided to cool down the sex image—for a while anyway. Her next public appearance found her in a demure suit of navy silk.

Marilyn's skyrocketing success spawned a slew of blonde, voluptuous knockoffs. Two of them, Jayne Mansfield and Sheree North, were signed and promoted by her own studio! Angered when Monroe walked out of her contract to study acting in New York, Fox hoped to threaten her with the two starlets. Though North soon dropped the Monroe image and developed into a fine actress, neither she nor Jayne possessed the singular Monroe magic. Mansfield in particular simply exaggerated Marilyn's sexy image while failing to temper it with anything approximating subtlety or elegance.

Here, Jayne Mansfield wears the gold pleated Travilla dress to the 1957 premiere of *The Spirit of St. Louis* in Hollywood. She and her husband, Mickey Hargitay, are being interviewed by Louis Quinn. Once again the neckline has been doctored. This time four small cords have been inserted across the plunging neckline to keep the more ample Mansfield bust in place.

William Travilla's final designing assignment was for the series *Dallas*. He produced versions of this gown for cast members Priscilla Presley and Victoria Principal. Recently, updates were seen on Naomi Watts, designed by Thierry Mugler, and on Elizabeth Hurley in a variation by Valentino. Nominated for her supporting role in *Doubt*, Viola Davis wore a similar design (with a fuller skirt) to the 2009 Oscar ceremonies.

WILLIAM TRAVILLA

This black satin full-length dress has straps encrusted with beads and drop crystals that merge into a deep "V" neckline. It is a typical studio costume in that it graced more than one star. Marilyn wore it for several sexy publicity portraits for *How to Marry a Millionaire*—but never onscreen—while Hildegard Knef slipped into it for a scene in *The Snows of Kilimanjaro*. A version of it was then seen on Ethel Merman in *There's No Business Like Show Business*. Crediting such a costume can be tricky. Travilla is listed as the designer of the Merman version, while Charles LeMaire and Sam Benson get credit for *The Snows of Kilimanjaro*. Studio designers were often frustrated by this one-style-fits-all policy, but they realized it came with the job.

BANG!

Soigné is the word for Marilyn in this costume test for *How to Marry a Millionaire*. As a fashion model with the unlikely name of Pola Debevoise, Monroe would be sharing the screen with Lauren Bacall and Betty Grable, whom she greatly admired.

This gown is a classic Travilla/Monroe product. It is made of deep magenta satin cut on the bias. Its single shoulder strap, worn close to the neck, leads to a diagonal swath that cuts under the bust line to Marilyn's left hip, where it then drops to a dramatic side train. Subtle embroidered beading sparkles on the shoulder strap and narrow belt. Monroe holds a matching wrap that she carried but never wore in the film.

How to Marry a Millionaire was only the second film to be made in Cinemascope. The three stars got wind of potentially unflattering distortions that could result from the process, and they were concerned about looking bulky on screen. In *Hollywood Costume Design*, David Chierichetti wrote: "Although the prevailing style of enormously full skirts made waistlines seem smaller, all three stars . . . refused to wear them. LeMaire [head of wardrobe] did not want Fox designers to appear ignorant of current fashion, so he called a meeting. Grable finally agreed to wear a cancan petticoat under a very full blue taffeta dress in the first scenes; Bacall wore a full-skirted printed shirt-waist in the fashion show [scene] and a couple of others flared; but Monroe was completely intransigent and insisted on tight skirts."

Travilla, of course, was well versed in Monroe's resistance to full skirts. As a designer of personal wardrobes for such fashion-conscious stars as Joan Crawford and Loretta Young, he tried occasionally to steer Marilyn away from her specific image. "Sex symbols can be difficult," he said, "because they know their appeal is based on just one thing and they have to keep that before the public at all times." Travilla and Charles LeMaire ended up sharing an Academy-Award nomination for the *Millionaire* costumes.

WILLIAM TRAVILLA

Pola arrives home from a night out in Manhattan. For this scene in *How to Marry a Millionaire*, Marilyn is wearing a fitted floor-length evening gown in cream wool cut on the bias. It is ornamented with cream and silver ribbon in a vermicular pattern. Silver ribbon adorns the wide-spaced shoulder straps and the self-belt. Several months earlier Marilyn wore the dress as she posed with handfuls of diamond jewelry for publicity photos to promote *Gentlemen Prefer Blondes*. This dress brought in $57,000 when auctioned by Christie's in the early 2000s.

perfect everything

A radiant Marilyn arrives for what she called "The happiest night of my life." It is the November 1953 premiere of *How to Marry a Millionaire* in Beverly Hills. In a theater packed with industry titans including Humphrey Bogart and Cecil B. DeMille, Monroe was applauded for reaching the peak of stardom. The recent success of

Niagara and *Gentlemen Prefer Blondes* guaranteed her top billing over veterans Bacall and Grable. Moreover, her self-deprecating comic performance in the film would delight critics.

When Monroe arrived at Fox early in the day to prepare for this auspicious occasion, she announced "I want to be all platinum and white tonight." (See page 159.) She was addressing her studio glamour squad: Travilla, hairstylist Gladys Rasmussen, and makeup man Alan "Whitey" Snyder. By the time she made a dazzling entrance at the premiere, nearly everything she wore was on loan from the studio. Travilla fashioned the gown in a sort of sexy fairy-princess style (from leftover material he used on a costume for June Haver in *The Girl Next Door*). It is white lace over nude crepe with the lace embellished by thousands of tiny opalescent sequins. A sash of white satin and a matching train added extra pizzazz. Marilyn had already been seen in the dress two months earlier when she made her TV debut on *The Jack Benny Show*. The gloves, earrings, shoes, and even the platinum polish on her finger and toenails were all property of Fox. The fur, an unusual combination of a muff on the end of a stole, was Marilyn's.

When this fabulous evening was over, Monroe had to report back to the studio where she was, like Cinderella, stripped of all of her glittering finery. She didn't care. The night had been a supreme triumph, capping years of hard work and dogged self-improvement.

In 1991 Madonna came close to recreating Marilyn's overall look here when she sang "Sooner or Later" from *Dick Tracy* on the Academy Awards telecast.

Marilyn and Lauren Bacall at the *Millionaire* premiere. Bacall, a former New York model, is the essence of sleek Manhattan style in her sequined Norman Norell sheath. By contrast, Marilyn personifies Hollywood excess. In just a couple of years Monroe would be living in New York and flaunting her curves in elegant Norell designs.

WILLIAM TRAVILLA

161

Monroe shares a laugh with Jack Carson at a 1954 benefit for the St. Jude Foundation. The silver lamé knife-pleated dress is halter topped and cut on the bias. Under the bodice, material twists to the waist and is anchored with a silver-and-pearl detail, then it drops to a tulip hemline.

I. LOVE. THEM. BOTH.

On the Fox lot in the summer of 1954, an amused Marilyn toasts Marlon Brando in full Napoleon regalia on the set of *Desirée*. Monroe has dropped by in costume from the set of *There's No Business Like Show Business*. This dress, a shade more *jeune fille* than the usual Monroe design is made of nylon tulle. It has ribbon shoulder straps and ribbon detailing under the bust. An appliquéd piece of feathery fabric (in a green abstract chrysanthemum pattern) covers the bodice and spills on to the top of the full skirt. It is repeated sporadically on the white skirt.

WILLIAM TRAVILLA

In a costume that fairly screams mid-century showbiz glitz, Marilyn poses on the set of *There's No Business Like Show Business*. She is about to join costars Ethel Merman, Dan Dailey, Donald O'Connor, Mitzi Gaynor, and Johnny Ray in the movies' title song/finale. As a nod to the well-known patriotism of Irving Berlin (the movie was built around his songs), Travilla put Merman in white, Gaynor in red, and Monroe in this blue showstopper.

The gown is made of Dupion silk with an overlay of tulle, cut on the bias. The drama comes from a mass of oval tulle petals in gradiating shades of blue that follow the bias from just below Marilyn's hipline to her ankles. Rather than rely on wire to frame the petals, Travilla had the tulle starched. This allowed for more fluidity of movement. The petals are trimmed in silver sequins and the body of the dress is embellished with dangling crystals of gradiating blue tones.

Costume sketch by Travilla

September 9, 1954, Monroe arrives in New York to begin filming locations for *The Seven Year Itch*. She is wearing a costume from *There's No Business Like Show Business*. It is a dress in beige "sheer wool "with a draped sewn-tie detail at the neck. A hem-length coat in the same fabric is lined in silk and features dramatic trim of honey-toned fox.

MARILYN in FASHION

Pretty in this pink silk pants and blouse ensemble with a cinch belt, Marilyn hits her mark in wide-band sandals that complete the summery look.

On another staircase
Marilyn models a costume
that the studio brass
felt was too risqué for
The Seven Year Itch.
The bare midriff top was
sleeveless, and the short
shorts were topped with
a soft leather belt that
featured an unusual detail
of tiny sewn-on buttons.

The hemline flounce on Travilla's costume sketch varies from the cotton eyelet dress Marilyn models in this *Seven Year Itch* costume test shot. Both versions had convertible straps that could be worn crisscrossed or in a halter style. Very few of these original Travilla sketches survived a fire in the 1970s that ravaged his studio. This one is from the Greg Schreiner collection.

WILLIAM TRAVILLA

This is the first photograph ever taken of Marilyn in the dress that would become the most famous in movie history.

For a brief scene in *The Seven Year Itch*, her character strolls on a Manhattan street on a stifling summer evening. When a subway rattles beneath her, Marilyn stands astride a sidewalk vent to catch a cool breeze that swirls her skirt up around her waist.

"I wanted her to look fresh and clean." Travilla recalled. "So I wondered what could I do with this most beautiful girl . . . to make her look talcum-powdered and adorable. What would I give her to wear that would blow in the breeze and be fun and pretty? I knew there would be a wind blowing so that would require a skirt."

The designer came up with a draped halter neck "fit-and-flair" dress cut on the bias in white rayon acetate with a pleated sunburst circle skirt. Wraparound ribbon-like bands support the bust and encircle the waist, leading to a self-tie that drops onto the left side of the skirt. Keen observers will note the modifications that took place after this test: Marilyn opted for a less structured hairstyle, and her earrings and shoes were replaced. Not surprisingly, the top of the dress was given a more flattering fit.

The "subway" scene was filmed on Lexington Avenue in midtown Manhattan late in the evening of September 15, 1954. It required several retakes in front of over two thousand gawking spectators and reporters. Disgusted by the spectacle, Joe DiMaggio walked off the location and soon thereafter out of his marriage.

The photographic images from that night—and from a studio version filmed later—continue to be some of the most reproduced in history. They struck a nerve immediately upon publication and signaled Monroe's ascension to pop culture queen. Even in the midst of the buttoned-down 1950s, few could resist the unique combination of creamy beauty, sexual allure, and playfulness that Monroe conveyed so naturally in this scene and the photographs it generated. (This shoot was one of the first in which a major star's exposed panties were showing in mainstream studio publicity.)

Copies of Travilla's deceptively simple masterpiece flew off the racks every summer for years, and new, modified versions continue to appear every couple of seasons. Travilla himself offered up a red version with deeper pleating in the skirt when he began a commercial line in the late '50s, and decades later Jean Paul Gaultier produced a "Baby Phat Yellow" variation for his affordable designs for Target department stores. In 1962, Fox

(not yet realizing the importance of the dress), reused it on actress Roxanne Arlen in the comedy *Bachelor Flat*. It was saved from further use by Debbie Reynolds, who acquired it at a Fox auction in the 1970s. In the last forty years, images of Monroe in the dress— even in silhouette—have become instantly recognizable symbols of Hollywood all over the world—as identifiable as the Hollywood sign itself.

Countless celebrities over the years have mimicked the dress and/or the scene. A small sampling: Donna Summer, Kelly LeBrock, Theresa Russell, Barbra Streisand, Julia Louis-Dreyfus, Mo'Nique, Katy Perry, and even Miss Piggy, and Smurfette. Every Halloween, tacky costume versions are seen on women, men, and lately even little girls. Sexy and daring in 1955, it has become as wholesome as apple pie.

Several years after the fact, Travilla made a duplicate that traveled in a show of his designs, but the original was housed safely among Debbie Reynolds' vast collection of movie memorabilia.

WILLIAM TRAVILLA

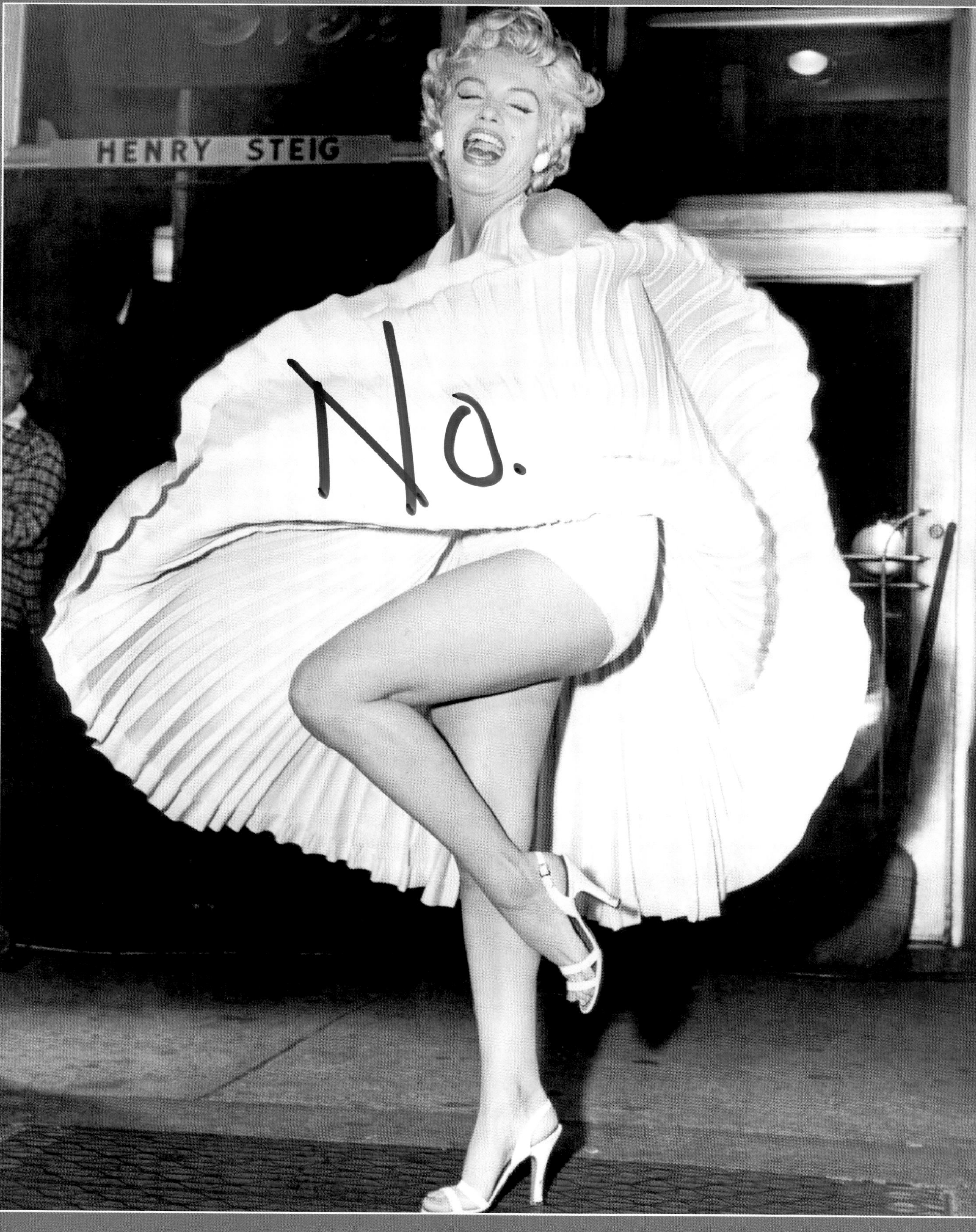
HENRY STEIG
No.

In June 2011, three events placed the dress in the news. On June 13, as the Duke and Duchess of Cambridge were visiting Canada, a gust from a helicopter at Calgary airport blew Kate Middleton's skirt up near her thighs. "Kate Middleton has Marilyn Monroe moment," read the *USA Today* headline. On June 18, Debbie Reynolds auctioned off the original dress for $5.6 million.

At the end of July, a twenty-six foot statue of Marilyn in the white dress with pleated skirt flying was unveiled in the Windy City. Located in the 400 block of Chicago's Michigan Avenue, the piece is the work of well-known American sculptor J. Seward Johnson, Jr. "There is something about her pose; the exuberance for life without inhibition," he remarked. The beautifully articulated statue became controversial when it was noted that people were standing directly under it to stare up at Marilyn's panties.

At the height of their collaboration Monroe inscribed a photo to William Travilla—and it wasn't just any photo. It was one of the graceful nudes taken by Tom Kelley in 1949. "To Billy My love—Please dress me forever. I love you, Marilyn." Forever lasted only until *Bus Stop* in 1956; Travilla designed the tacky showgirl costume in which Marilyn sings "That Old Black Magic." Her other costumes for the film were pulled from the Fox wardrobe department. For whatever reason, Monroe did not request Travilla for *Let's Make Love* when she returned to Fox in 1960 after two loan-outs to other studios.

WILLIAM TRAVILLA

MISCELLANEOUS
DESIGNERS

∾

Everything.

In her Hollywood apartment studying sheet music for a song she never recorded, Marilyn is in a wool skirt with a side kick pleat, black open-toed pumps and a lively print blouse by Dorothy Cox for McMullen.

Shortly after her separation from Joe DiMaggio in the fall of 1954, Marilyn posed for these charming shots in the Ferndell section of L.A.'s Griffith Park. The black and white sleeveless sweater dress with a cowl neck is by Walter Bass (for whom future fashion legend Rudi Gernreich was designing at the time), and is typical of the classic sportswear Monroe was drawn to for casual times. In this respect her taste was not unlike that of Grace Kelly, Audrey Hepburn, and Doris Day, contemporaries with more ladylike images. Walter Bass became known for the up-to-the minute sporty styles he placed on Mary Tyler Moore for her starring role on *The Dick Van Dyke Show*.

MARILYN IN FASHION

STRIPES.

The outfit pictured here is more in the traditional Monroe mold. The loose-fitting olive green top matched her eyes. It is given panache with the turned-up collar and plunging neckline. Candy-striped pedal pushers in the same green, cream, and pumpkin complete the ensemble.

Monroe's favorite casual outfit was even simpler. At home, she liked nothing better than to snuggle in a lush white terry cloth robe. She wore them sans undergarments, of course, and even conducted print interviews in them. She had a standing order for the robes at Bullocks Wilshire, where they cost $18.67 each.

Despite the public's perception of her as a glamour doll, Marilyn was always relieved to be able to dress down for life outside the studio gates. Although she basked in the excitement the Monroe persona provoked in her public life, Marilyn was, of course, still Norma Jeane. "A more playful, natural person," wrote Meredith Etherington-Smith, "who liked cracking jokes, having fun, hanging out anonymously with friends . . . in neighborhood bars."

Marilyn chose this Nardiello suit in black wool to return to Hollywood in triumph from New York. Twentieth Century Fox acceded to her financial and artistic demands, renewed her contract, and cast her in *Bus Stop*, to be based on the smash Broadway play. She gave a brief press conference upon her arrival at Los Angeles International airport on February 26, 1956. The suit is in business-like black wool with a black satin shirt and matching necktie. Marilyn wore the suit with black leather gloves and matching pumps. The over-all effect was of a young woman very much in charge.

When one reporter said, "You're wearing a high-necked dress now. Last time I saw you, you weren't. Is this a new Marilyn?" After a short pause, Monroe got laughs when she replied, "No, I'm the same person, but it's a different suit."

East of Eden.

♡ JAMES DEAN

James didn't care for Marilyn, though they never met...

the best of us...

Designer George Nardiello met Marilyn through Milton Greene shortly after her arrival in New York in 1955. For the next few years, he and John Moore, both graduates of Parsons School of Design, worked with her closely, sometimes in collaboration with Norman Norell. Nardiello had mixed feelings about Marilyn. In a 1991 interview he told Scott Eyman, "She was very difficult to design for because she wanted everything to look like a slip. Everything had to be skintight; you had to reinforce every seam or everything would break." Asked if she had good taste, he responded, "No. She was like Joan Crawford; you had to tell her what to wear." By 2003, Nardiello had softened, telling *The Palm Beach Post*, "Monroe was heavenly to dress. She looked even more gorgeous without any makeup on, sitting around in this beat-up terry-cloth bathrobe. I used to make her pancakes with caviar and sour cream."

For the March 1955 New York premiere of *East of Eden*, Monroe wore this long champagne-toned brocade sheath with fishtail back detail and a matching fox-trimmed wrap. Accessorized by white gloves, it was a tasteful design, but the snug fit gave it the sexy glamour Marilyn knew her public expected. Though Norell has been suggested as the designer, he never worked in brocade at this time. It is most likely a Nardiello.

In March 1956, Marilyn held a casual press party. She is wearing Nardiello's black version* of Norell's satin cocktail dress she wore in January 1955. This would become a habit of Marilyn's, having an original design copied (usually by a designer of lesser stature or a Seventh Avenue dressmaker) in a number of colors, fabrics, and even different sizes to accommodate her weight fluctuations. There is no public indication that any of her designers objected to this practice.

*This dress now resides in the Wayne Murray collection.

Arthur Miller and
Marilyn emerge
from a screening
of *Some Like It Hot*
in February 1959.
Monroe is in a
tailored suit of
charcoal gray fine
wool with long
sleeves and trimmed
in a deep fox-fur
collar. It is by Irene
for Gunther Jaeckel,
New York. For a
brief time as Marilyn
was promoting
this classic comedy
which contained
one of her sexiest
performances, she
ironically took on
a slightly matronly
appearance with
her choice of suits,
dresses, and even
hairstyles and jewelry.

MARILYN ɪɴ FASHION

March 5, 1961: Marilyn's press representative, Pat Newcomb, guides her through reporters as she leaves the Columbia Presbyterian Medical Hospital in Manhattan. She is dressed in a cashmere twin-set by Bonnie Cashin.

It can't be denied that some critics found Marilyn vulgar in certain photo spreads and even (though rarely) on screen. This 1952 portrait would bolster their opinions. The gown is a strapless knit sheath with a sweetheart neckline outlined in fake fur. A draping detail draws the eye to, well . . . Monroe's crotch. Her expression adds to the obviousness of the whole image. No designer credit can be found for this gown. If it is William Travilla's as some propose, it certainly lacks his usual taste.

UNKNOWN DESIGNERS

In Japan on their honeymoon in January 1954, the DiMaggios enjoy meeting some locals. Marilyn is appropriately dressed down in a jumper of tan rayon jersey over a mock turtleneck top with cap sleeves. The elastic cinch belt with a metal clasp was a mainstay of 1950s fashion. Marilyn's headscarf was one she wore repeatedly.

April 16, 1954: Marilyn charms reporters upon her return to Twentieth Century Fox after her elongated honeymoon. She is in a rib knit sleeveless boat neck sheath in a burnt orange, accessorized with a black belt and sideless open-toed pumps. The earrings are ones she would soon wear in *The Seven Year Itch* with the white dress.

Marilyn and Arthur Miller dash to a waiting train at Washington, D.C.'s Union Station on May 23, 1957. They are headed back to New York after the conclusion of Miller's trial for contempt of court.* Monroe heeds the call for "Just one more, Marilyn!" from photographers. Her dress is tan and white striped sleeveless cotton. It has tan trim around the neck and back of the arms, an elastic waistband, and a back kick pleat. Based on the color scheme, this may be a John Moore design, but it can't be verified.

*Miller had refused to give names of alleged Communist writers with whom he had attended five or six meetings in Manhattan in 1945. In 1958, he was cleared of the charges.

PART TWO

A FASHIONABLE
MISCELLANY

THE MAKEUP DEPARTMENT

Marilyn touches up her lipstick during a Manhattan cocktail party in her honor. She was being welcomed to New York for location filming on *The Seven Year Itch* in early September 1954.

Stories are legion about Monroe fussing at her makeup mirror for upwards of two hours as she prepared for a public appearance or before reporting to a movie set or even just for a date. Less sympathetic journalists—and coworkers who were forced to wait for her—saw this habit as towering self absorption. It was, of course, but it was not necessarily rooted in narcissism. It had begun when she was still a teenager. "She was a perfectionist about her appearance," recalled her first husband, James Dougherty. "If anything she was too critical of herself."

Becoming world renowned for her facial beauty failed to increase her confidence. "Marilyn has to steel herself for an encounter with reality," wrote Jim Henaghan in 1953 for *Motion Picture*. "She does this . . . by stalling as long as possible and by trying to look her best."

THE MAKEUP DEPARTMENT

As a model Marilyn had learned to do a superb job with her makeup. When she reached stardom, she gave wise advice in fan magazines that she didn't always follow herself. "When a man looks into your eyes, he doesn't like looking into an over-heavy mess of mascara and eye shadow," she told *Photoplay* in October 1953. In these 1952 portraits, with the over-drawn upper lip and the obvious false lashes, Monroe's makeup is a holdover from the 1940s.

The late Anne Francis began her Fox contract in 1952 and she observed Marilyn at various times on the lot. "She really was like two different people," Francis said in 1978. "That's not an exaggeration. One time she would be over-made up, and every movement was calculated to push the sex image. The next time she would be clean scrubbed—maybe just wearing a little pale lipstick—down to earth and terribly sweet. And I thought she was much lovelier without the heavy makeup; it could actually distract from the natural beauty she was blessed with. As her career solidified, she learned to tone it down."

In London on November 19, 1956, Marilyn in minimal makeup, concentrates on a staged debate about the state of British theater at the Royal Court Theatre, while audience members concentrate on her. She was there not to call attention to herself but because Arthur Miller was on the debate panel. Still, the British press jibed that she "looks anything but glamorous with hair [that] is very unruly."

Though she was never nominated for an Oscar, Marilyn did receive recognition from film academies in France and Italy, and from the Hollywood Foreign Press Association. Here, in March 1960, she had just received a Golden Globe for her lustrous performance in *Some Like It Hot*.

Cradled in a cloud of white fox with minimal makeup and a soft hairstyle, she looks younger than she did a decade earlier. She was in the midst of filming *Let's Make Love*. Months later when the film came out, the *Time* magazine critic said, "At 34, she makes 21 look ridiculous."

This is the less-is-more look Marilyn now favored, though she realized her image would often dictate more heightened glamour. "Flashy earrings, necklaces, and bracelets detract from a lady's looks," she said. "And even if I have to wear that stuff, I don't have to own it. The studio lends it to me whenever they want to show me off." In 1985 hairstylist George Masters recalled, "Marilyn Monroe always turned her back to the mirror then looked around. Whatever she saw first—eyes or lips—she would tone down."

Prior to the premiere of *How to Marry a Millionaire* in the fall of 1953, Monroe adds a finishing touch. Her favorite makeup man, Alan "Whitey" Snyder, looks on. "Marilyn has makeup tricks that nobody else has and nobody knows," Snyder told author Maurice Zolotow. "Some of them she won't even tell me. She discovered them herself. She has certain ways of lining and shadowing her eyes that no other actress can do. She puts on a special kind of lipstick; it's a secret blend of three different shades. I get that moist look on her lips . . . by first putting on lipstick and then putting gloss over the lipstick." If gloss [not yet manufactured commercially] wasn't handy, Monroe would make do with a thin layer of Vaseline over her lips.

False eyelashes were another Monroe specialty. She would cut them in half and wear them only at the out-side corner of her lids—getting that desired uplift while still looking natural. The beauty mark came and went depending on Marilyn's mood or if it was appropriate for a movie role. It was, however, not a phony. It was a small colorless mole that she could easily conceal or darken for effect. Sometimes she would cover the real thing and draw one on, as she did for *Some Like It Hot*, wearing it on her chin as the flappers of the '20s did.

MARILYN in FASHION

Marilyn's favorite studio hairstylist in the early 1950s was Gladys Rasmussen. "There are several problems in doing Marilyn's hair," she said in 1960. "Her hair is very fine and therefore hard to manage. It gets very oily if it isn't shampooed every day. And, her hair is so curly naturally that to build a coiffure for her I have to first give her a straight permanent." Here, during a publicity trip to the east coast, Marilyn doesn't mind a photographer capturing her as she waits for Gladys to do her magic.

After napping on a flight from Los Angeles in 1956, Monroe is unconcerned about her messy hair as she offers a winning smile for the press. Marilyn was the first star of any magnitude to appear in public unconcerned about the state of her tresses. She often dressed to the nines but kept her hair a little mussed. It's as if she were declaring, "All of this beauty is just thrown together, I don't really spend much time on it." Maybe she thought she was countering all the tales about the hours spent in front of her makeup mirror. There was also a winking suggestion of sexuality in looking like she just rolled out of bed. Today "bed head" or "morning after" hair is common, but when Marilyn wore it she raised eyebrows.

THE MAKEUP DEPARTMENT

Speaking of eyebrows, this shot taken just prior to Monroe filming the studio version of the subway-grating scene in *The Seven Year Itch*, shows off the beautifully arched natural brows that framed her eyes so effectively. She liked an "architectural" shape to her brows and, interestingly, she darkened them as she lightened her hair over the years.

At columnist Walter Winchell's 1953 birthday party in Hollywood, Marilyn radiates health and sex appeal. The glow is partially thanks to one of her makeup tricks. She would apply a dab of Vaseline on her cheekbones and on the bone under her eyebrow to add a glisten to her skin and highlight her bone structure.

THE MAKEUP DEPARTMENT

THE
HAIR SALON

A hairdo test photo from *Gentlemen Prefer Blondes* has Marilyn modeling artificial bangs. She ended up wearing a version of this style in the movie, but with a different costume. It was for a hilarious scene in which she locks herself into a stateroom and has to exit out of the porthole.

Marilyn poses as seductive Angela in one of her first important films, the classic 1950 John Huston crime drama *The Asphalt Jungle*. On the MGM lot, Marilyn fell into the gifted hands of legendary Sidney Guilaroff, the studio's chief hairstylist since 1937. In a career that eventually spanned nearly sixty years, he styled everyone from Jeanette MacDonald to Liza Minnelli.

Lana Turner (right) was the top blonde at MGM, so it's not surprising that the studio imposed the Turner image on Marilyn when it came to shoot *Asphalt Jungle* publicity photos. The Monroe poses are reminiscent of Turner shots used to promote the 1943 comedy *Slightly Dangerous*. (Marilyn's black dress had been designed by Irene for Lucille Bremer to wear in *Yolanda and the Thief* in 1945.)

In 1995, Sidney Guilaroff said, "When I first saw Marilyn, I felt she was wearing her hair too long. She resisted cutting it at first, but I convinced her that a shorter style would flatter her bone structure and bring out her lovely facial features, which of course it did."

Monroe offers a pretty pout in a 1953 portrait taken for print ads touting Westmore's "close-up" lipstick and "tru-glow" liquid makeup. Marilyn also appeared in Lustre Crème shampoo ads. It was not considered déclassé for even the biggest stars to do these commercial tie-ins, just as no one bats an eye half a century later when they see Drew Barrymore hawking Cover Girl.

favorite!

After reaching superstardom, Marilyn wore her hair noticeably longer than usual only twice. Here in 1953, she is caught by surprise it seems at her Canadian hotel room on location for *River of No Return*. This was when her romance with Joe DiMaggio was really heating up. The second time was during her marriage to Arthur Miller in 1957. Since men often prefer longer hair, it's not too farfetched (though not recorded anywhere), to imagine that Monroe grew her hair to please the men in her life at the time.

THE HAIR SALON

In 1959–60, wigs became fashionable (and affordable) for street wear for the first time in decades. The bouffant styles lent themselves to being recreated in wig form, and Marilyn turned to them more than once for the next couple of years.

When looking for a hairstyle to help her define Roslyn in *The Misfits*, Marilyn looked to Sidney Guilaroff for the first time in a decade. In Manhattan in the summer of 1960 prior to the start of filming, Monroe modeled these wigs of his design. They are both departures from the shorter styles she had worn in her last two films, but the one with the bangs and the modified "flip" styling was more youthful and it's the one Marilyn chose.

Guilaroff designed this style and the others Marilyn wore in the film, but it was Agnes Flanagan who served as Monroe's hairdresser on location in Nevada, just as she had on *Some Like It Hot*. Flanagan and Monroe went all the way back to *The Fireball* in 1950, and they worked together often up to the time of Marilyn's death. Flanagan had the sad responsibility of styling the Guilaroff *Misfits* wig Marilyn wore for her funeral service.

Marilyn's beauty is captured as if in a portrait in this candid shot from 1961. She is leaving St. Cyril's Catholic Church in Encino, California on June 22, 1961, having just attended the star-studded christening of Clark Gable's son. A net scarf with a motif of hearts obscures her wig.

At a party in Hollywood in 1958 just prior to the start of *Some Like It Hot* filming, Monroe was greeted by Louella Parsons: "Your hair is platinum now," she said. "Oh no," Marilyn replied, "It's white hot! For my picture *Some Like It Hot*."

Kenneth Battelle of the Lily Daché millinery and hair salon in New York prepares Marilyn's hair for the 1959 Chicago premiere of *Some Like It Hot* in March 1959. Norman Norell introduced Marilyn to Battelle and he brought her into the bouffant era. Erroneously called Mr. Kenneth by the press, Battelle remains the only hairstylist to win a Coty award. He had been Jacqueline Kennedy's favorite hairdresser since 1954, and he also tended the manes of Lauren Bacall, Audrey Hepburn, and Judy Garland. He became Marilyn's primary stylist when in New York.

"Of all my steady clients," he told *Architectural Digest* in 2004, "Marilyn was the one who was truly my friend. . . . Of course she kept me waiting—to know her was to wait. For three or four hours sometimes . . . But I counted on it, and I allowed for it—and I never minded. Just before she died, she called me from a pay phone. She said she was on the highway somewhere, driving around, and that she just wanted to hear my voice. All in that breathy, little-girl tone she had. But you know something, Jackie talked softer than Marilyn."

Marilyn looks pensive in this moment from the 1962 Golden Globe Awards at the Beverly Hills Hotel. She is wearing a new coiffure by brash young California stylist George Masters. Based at the Saks Fifth Avenue salon in Beverly Hills, Masters courted press attention in part by going after established stylists like Battelle. "Mrs. Kennedy wears her hair too big," he told one columnist. Masters named Cyd Charisse and Lynda Bird Johnson among his clients, but Marilyn was always the star of any of his interviews. "It took me hours to get her all pulled together," he told the Los Angeles *Times* in 1977. "But eventually, when she was set to go—pow! She exploded."

For the last year of her life, Masters and Agnes Flanagan shared duties as Marilyn's west coast stylists.

Kenneth Battelle styled Marilyn's hair for one of her most famous appearances, on March 19, 1962. Knowing she wanted to project larger-than-life glamour at Madison Square Garden when singing "Happy Birthday" to President John Kennedy, Battelle exaggerated her familiar bell-shaped hairdo by adding a sweeping wing-bang over her right eye. It was a hairstyle that had a significant afterlife. As the '60s progressed, and the so-called "generation gap" widened, many young girls discarded lacquered bouffant hairdos in favor of hair worn long and straight, or in Sassoon-esque geometrical bobs. Mature women, unable to follow those trends, wanted something they would feel comfortable wearing, but which also lent them a touch of glamour. As a result, variations of Monroe's "do" from Madison Square Garden were seen on women of various ages for almost two decades.

"When Marilyn wore that style," says Richard Parker, formerly of the Beverly Hills Hotel salon, "with that dramatic bang, it looked so new. But within just a few years, it became a cliché on legions of older gals."

TOPPING
IT OFF

A photo spread entitled "Milady's Easter Bonnet" in an April 1958 issue of *American Weekly* magazine featured hats worn by a group including Marilyn, Eleanor Roosevelt, Mamie Eisenhower, and Lucille Ball.

This hat of Italian straw and cascading roses is the creation of Laddie Northridge of the Lord and Taylor salon. "Marilyn Monroe is the feminine symbol of our time," Northridge said. This is a style Marilyn would never have worn if not for a photo shoot. She did buy straw hats from the Northridge salon, but nothing this elaborate. For film roles, of course, she was agreeable to whatever headgear was deemed proper for her character, but off screen she favored going bareheaded. When her hair was not up to snuff, she preferred wearing a scarf. She did, however, hide under a variety of shapeless hats when she didn't want to be recognized.

On the rare occasion when Monroe would buy a hat for her personal use, rather than grab one from studio wardrobe, she would turn to the Jay Thorpe, Adolfo, or Mr. John salons in Manhattan, or to Rex of Beverly Hills. Her favorite style was the classic beret. She wore flattering variations of it off screen and in eight films, from *Ladies of the Chorus* in 1949 through *Something's Got to Give* in 1962. She always wore them high on the right side of her head, and with few exceptions, they were always in black.

Young sweethearts, Marilyn and Rand Brooks appear in a backstage scene from *Ladies of the Chorus*. This was Monroe's first substantive role. The beret, courtesy of the Columbia Pictures wardrobe department, is in the floppy Rembrandt tradition.

MARILYN IN FASHION

Marilyn is surely the world's most elegant football fan in this 1951 portrait used for print advertisements for the new "Stadium Styles" from City Club men's shoes.

Monroe's black beret contrasts with costar Jane Russell's pink brocade sailor-like hat in this moment from *Gentlemen Prefer Blondes*. These hats—and all the *chapeaux* worn in the stylish musical comedy—were from famed New York designer Mr. John.

Going without her eyeglasses but not her beret, Marilyn as a myopic fashion model captures the heart of David Wayne in this scene from *How to Marry a Millionaire*.

Beneath still another beret, Monroe signs an autograph in the midst of her whirlwind tour of Korean military bases in February 1954.

Her final public appearance and her final beret: Marilyn wears a lush mink beret on June 1, 1962.

Don't
WORRY.
EVER.

Marilyn is at her prettiest just prior to a performance that unfortunately no one will see. She is at the NBC radio studio in Hollywood for an August 31, 1952 broadcast of the original story, "Statement in Full." She is wearing a favorite scarf in red and ivory that she wore again on location for *River of No Return* and again on her honeymoon in Japan.

TOPPING IT OFF

The chalkboard reads:

NEWMAN A635
MARILYN MONROE
AS "ROBERTA"
CH #2
EXT. SCOTT
HOUSE- 67, 69

4/5/51   DES
              RENIE

For her entrance in *Love Nest*, Renié finished off Marilyn's suit with a sharp black and white hat that she topped with a long, dramatic black feather.

By the time filming began, the feather was gone and a spotted veil had been added.

More than a year and a half after *Love Nest*, Marilyn is photographed before hopping a plane to New York wearing the hat, but now *sans* veil and finished with a feather placed at a less dangerous angle. As was so often the case, she is dressed head to toe in studio wardrobe. The suit in two-tone gray linen was a Charles LeMaire design that had been seen in 1951 on Jeanne Crain in *Take Care of My Little Girl*.

MARILYN in FASHION

Marilyn offers a pose at a New York airport as she awaits a flight to Jamaica in the lounge in January 1957. This is one of the few times when she got everything wrong. The dress is too tight, the pose forced, the gloves are ugly, and the hair is messy without any flair. Worst is the silly hat that resembles an inverted knit flowerpot.

At the Half Moon resort in Montego Bay, Mr. and Mrs. Arthur Miller look like any couple on vacation. Marilyn is wearing a small brimmed fur felt hat for protection from the Jamaican sun. Contrasted with the picture taken in the airport, Monroe is just being herself, not feeling the need to project the public M.M. image.

TOPPING IT OFF

Marilyn gives the photographer a seductive glance under a Garbo-esque black unblocked felt hat from the Laddie

perfect always & forever.

In a Manhattan studio, a demure Marilyn models a Jean Louis costume and hat for a test of clothes for *The Misfits*. By the time the scene was filmed in Reno, Marilyn wore the veil pushed nearly to the back of her head.

Arriving in Nevada after a short hospital stay in Los Angeles, Marilyn returns to *The Misfits* production in September 1960. She is wearing an unusual outfit that includes a straw boater with an attached scarf.

Marilyn seldom wore fussy or oversized hats that would distract from her blonde beauty, but she had another reason for avoiding such styles; "I have a very big head you know," she once joked to a costumer, "nothing in it of course, but a big head."

TOPPING IT OFF

KEEPING
COZY

Jack Benny gets a laugh
from Marilyn as she and
the comedian leave a
Hollywood rehearsal on
September 11, 1953 for
his television show, to be
broadcast two days later.
She is wearing a luxurious
camel hair overcoat with
an oversized buckle by
Christian Dior.

Marilyn accompanies Tommy Rettig (her costar in the just completed *River of No Return*) to the premiere of his new movie, *The 5,000 Fingers of Dr. T* on October 11, 1953. Marilyn is wearing a black satin three-quarter gown, matched by black gloves and black open-toed pumps, the better to set off the glamorous evening coat. It is a collarless update of a 1920s clutch coat in white cashmere. The matching fox fur cuffs were detachable. Although the gown seemed fairly conservative, when photographers asked Marilyn to remove the coat, she couldn't help but tease, saying it would be "too extreme" in the presence of a young boy.

Shortly before their marriage, Marilyn and Joe DiMaggio are photographed with her wearing the brown ranch full-length mink coat he gave her as an early wedding gift. This was one of the few furs that Monroe actually owned. She usually borrowed them from the studio for special occasions. Joe also gave her an eternity ring consisting of thirty-five baguette-cut diamonds and a strand of pearls he bought for her on their honeymoon in Japan. In 1999 the ring (minus one stone) brought $772,500 at an auction of her effects at Christie's.

July 13, 1956: The Millers are about to board a plane to London for filming on *The Prince and the Showgirl*. Over her beige John Moore sheath, Marilyn is wearing a favorite white silk trench coat.

Candle in the wind...

Two days later, at the conclusion of her press conference at the Savoy hotel in London, Marilyn in a trendsetting Galanos dress, is helped into her loose fitting double-breasted evening coat of ivory satin. It fastens with mother of pearl buttons and is decorated by wide lapels.

Marilyn models a Dorothy Jeakins designed coat in black and white check for *Let's Make Love*. It is in wool and features patch pockets, a rolled black collar, and large matching cuffs.

On June 15, 1961, a fresh-faced Marilyn arrives in New York wearing a blue and white jersey coat woven in a modified lattice pattern. It is lined with silk, has three contrasting buttons, and patch pockets. The label reads Women's Haberdashers. Under the coat she wears a green Pucci sheath.

MARILYN IN ENGLAND

Accompanied by her new husband, Arthur Miller, Marilyn caused a sensation when she arrived in London in July 1956 to film *The Prince and the Showgirl*. The comedy set in 1911 was to costar and be directed by Laurence Olivier.

For the first photo opportunity of the Millers posing with Olivier and his wife, Vivien Leigh, Marilyn wore this John Moore design in beige silk. The high-necked sheath with medium-length sleeves is saved from plainness by the way in which it flatters Monroe's bustline. The banding Moore placed so snugly under the bodice as built-in support for her breasts gives the design the uplift that Monroe loved, allowing her to go *sans* brassiere.

At a July 15 press conference at the Savoy Hotel, Marilyn was radiant in this black Galanos. A 1956 winner of the Coty award, young Philadelphia native James Galanos was already a name to be reckoned with. Noted for his artful handling of chiffon, he was also dedicated to designing the "perfect black dress." He came close with this cocktail number in wool crepe. The crisp design is given a stroke of the provocative with a bare midriff covered in chiffon. Marilyn knew the dress spoke for itself so she downplayed the accessories. In January 1957, the Associated Press reported, "Marilyn sets British style trend. [The] peek-a-boo midriff note set by Marilyn Monroe . . . last summer has won the approval of London style setters. No one less than Queen Elizabeth's own dressmaker, Norman Hartnell, yesterday showed a bare-but-veiled midriff number as part of his spring collection." Galanos would become a major American designer. In 1981 fashion critics raved about his glittery, one-shoulder gown that Nancy Reagan chose for her husband's Inaugural ball.

MARILYN IN FASHION

On October 12, Monroe gave the press and public what they had been craving—red-hot glamour. For the West End premiere of Arthur Miller's hit play, *A View from the Bridge*, she squeezed into this crimson velvet fishtail gown. "Marilyn Monroe's close-fitting dress turned the London opening into a near riot," wrote the Associated Press. The strapless, chest-baring bodice was in a complementary red satin, as was a luxurious stole lined in brown mink. Open-toed platform heels dyed to match the satin created a statuesque impression. When reporters asked Miller if he felt his wife should have worn something simple (in black for instance) so as not to steal his spotlight, he laughed: "Why should someone like Marilyn pretend to be dressing like somebody's old aunt?"

Marilyn said she chose the dress because red was Arthur's favorite color. The girl who wore black all the time in the States added, "I'm a movie star. If I were in black it wouldn't be me."

Unfortunately, the designer of this sumptuous and controversial gown has been lost to time. It is possible it was the work of Beatrice Dawson, her designer on *The Prince and the Showgirl*. During production, Marilyn grew close to Dawson. When not needed on the film set, she and Marilyn spent several afternoons shopping at Harrods, Marks & Spencer, and other London salons. During one of these sojourns, Marilyn chose the gown she would wear later in the month to meet Queen Elizabeth II.

We know for certain that she acquired the platform shoes at Anello & Davide in Covent Garden. Platform heels had not been fashionable since the 1940s, when Carmen Miranda made them popular. Anello & Davide, however, still produced them for theatrical productions. The venerable shoemakers would gain fame a decade later when their Cuban-heeled, short-topped boots were made famous by the Beatles.

MARILYN IN ENGLAND

Elizabeth II meets Marilyn Monroe as actor Victor Mature looks on. It is late October 1956, and Marilyn is in the final weeks of filming *The Prince and the Showgirl*. This goddess-like ensemble is in a burnished gold lamé. The figure-hugging gown featured barely visible spaghetti straps, and was accessorized with a matching opera cape and elbow-length gloves in soft ochre. Another pair of platform shoes gave her added height.

Not surprisingly, Marilyn chose to discard the cape for her actual presentation, thereby placing her creamy décolletage on full display. The Queen didn't seem to take offense, however, and the two women exchanged pleasantries. Perhaps Marilyn got away with the gown because she otherwise appeared so understated. Her hair color and makeup were toned down for her role in *Showgirl*, and this more natural look helped balance the effect of her neckline.

The British press, however, screamed that she should have dressed more conservatively. Singer Jane Morgan, also present at the event, agreed. She said Monroe's dress was made of "gold tissue," and she pointed out that all of the female attendees including Brigitte Bardot, Anita Ekberg, and Joan Crawford had been admonished to dress conservatively, and all complied except Monroe. Talking to *Life* magazine a year later, Marilyn said, "If I had abided by the rules I never would have gotten anywhere."

OFF
THE RACK

After giving eye-catching supporting performances in *The Asphalt Jungle* and *All About Eve*, Twentieth Century Fox studio chief Darryl F. Zanuck placed Marilyn under contract in 1951. Her first contract with the studio signed in 1946 led nowhere. This time she was promised a big build-up.

With a steady paycheck coming in, she indulged in some new clothes. She bought this evening gown at I. Magnin's department store. It is a strapless red silk taffeta, snug from the bodice down to just below the hips, and covered in black French lace. The taffeta underskirt is finished with a ruched balloon hemline. The black lace gloves and a black fox boa Marilyn usually wore with the dress helped soften some of its gaudiness. "I paid a stiff price for it," Marilyn said. "I was told that the dress was the only copy of an original purchased by a San Francisco social leader."

Marilyn wore the dress on several occasions, including the 1952 *Photoplay* magazine awards, and for the party celebrating the opening of *Don't Bother to Knock*. She considered it her lucky dress because of the attention it always brought her although it was criticized in the press. "This was the dress that provoked so much comment . . . it was proof positive, they claimed that I was utterly lacking in taste. I'm truly sorry, but I love the dress."

Unlike many glamour girls from the studio era who wouldn't have dreamed of buying off the rack once they reached stardom, Marilyn was never a snob about clothes. As the top box-office draw in Hollywood, if she saw a dress in a modest neighborhood shop, she wouldn't hesitate to buy it. Whether it cost $1,800 or $18, she didn't care as long as the piece was well made and flattering.

In September 1955, Marilyn lent her potent presence to the opening of an exhibit honoring Abraham Lincoln in the town of Bement, Illinois. The sixteenth president was a personal hero of Monroe's and she agreed to a number of events in his honor, including serving as judge for a Lincoln-like beard contest. She is in a day dress of white lace over an under dress of baby blue. Though she was wearing white spring-o-lator shoes, she carried a black patent-leather clutch and black gloves.

Two years later for a photo series of Monroe exploring various locations in Brooklyn and Manhattan, she chose this white cotton sundress. Saw-tooth detailing accents the armholes and scoop neckline. This dress reportedly cost $5.98.

Mr. and Mrs. Arthur Miller enter their 57th Street apartment. It is August 1957, and Marilyn has just been discharged from New York's Doctor's Hospital following a miscarriage. In spite of her sad ordeal, Marilyn is radiant and offers a wan smile for the press. She and Arthur had been enjoying the summer at a seaside home in quaint Amagansett on Long Island. The dress is one Marilyn most likely bought in the Hamptons. She enjoyed shopping at the little local boutiques she discovered there or when she visited Connecticut. The dress is a double layer of white lace with incorporated shoulder straps and a slim self-belt. The full skirt was an unusual choice for Marilyn. A month earlier, she wowed the crowd in the dress at the ground-breaking ceremony for the Time-Life Building, across the street from Rockefeller Center.

MARILYN IN FASHION

Monroe is exuberant on July 8, 1958 as she boards a plane at New York's Idlewild Airport.
She is headed to Hollywood to film *Some Like It Hot*. The white silk set has a charmeuse skirt.

Three days later, at the Beverly Hills Hotel, Marilyn poses at a press reception toasting the start of *Some Like It Hot* production. The dress is in black silk crepe with dolman sleeves. Below the bodice the material is gathered in the front (a nod to vintage Hattie Carnegie style lines), and drapes down to a "pouf hemline." The plunging neckline is matched in the back. So that it wouldn't be put on backwards, there was a "Front" label sewn in. The dress was the product of the Manor-Bourne line, and Marilyn purchased it at her favorite West Coast store, I. Magnin's. In May 2011, this dress sold at auction for $338,000.

At Idlewild again, Marilyn poses in early July 1960. She is on her way to Los Angeles, then Reno for filming on *The Misfits*. The caption, courtesy of American Airlines, says she is "wearing a light tan sport outfit." It is actually beige, with a men's style shirt in a subtle stripe and a linen-like cotton skirt from Jax on 57th Street. The belt and pumps were ones Monroe wore often. In 1953 she told *Modern Screen*, "I only have a few idiosyncrasies about clothes. I like bare-looking shoes for both formal and informal occasions. I believe, like the classic Greeks, that a woman's feet are an important part of her beauty." Marilyn also chose pumps in bone because she felt they gave the impression of lengthening her legs.

OUT OF
THE CLOSET

Low budget films often required actors to supply their own wardrobe, and Marilyn was no exception in a few of her early movie appearances. In 1949, for her memorable walk-on opposite Groucho Marx in *Love Happy*, she wore this floor-length, figure-hugging strapless gown in gold lamé. It featured a front slit from knee to hem that was obscured by a cascading self-sash near the left hip. Marilyn wore it with gold ankle-strap platform heels.

Pin-Up Superstar

She first donned the gown in 1948 for a modeling assignment with pinup photographer Earl Moran, and several months later for a rare invitation-only nightclub performance at the Florentine Gardens in Hollywood (seen here with musician Phil Moore).

Marilyn's overall look in this shimmering number owes a nod to the prevailing Hollywood image of glamour—Rita Hayworth as *Gilda*. Not surprisingly, Marilyn pushed the sex impact for her version. The fabric was sheer enough so that when stretched a bit over her breasts, it revealed the outline of her nipples.

For two 1950 cheapies, *Hometown Story* (above with Alan Hale, Jr.) and *The Fireball* (a Mickey Rooney vehicle), Marilyn chose this wool sweater dress in tan and black with a mock turtleneck. Whenever she wore this design on or off screen, she turned down the collar and fastened it with a pin—a detail that called attention to her face. (She wore the dress a third time for a 1950 screen test that clinched her contract with Twentieth Century Fox. She acted opposite Richard Conte in a scene from *Cold Shoulder*, a proposed gangster movie.)

For another scene in *Fireball* with Mickey Rooney, Marilyn wore her most conservative suit in navy wool with a stone marten fur wrap and her favorite pair of scallop-topped, open-toed pumps. "The first expensive clothes I ever owned," Marilyn said in 1952, "were the three suits which I bought on credit from a Hollywood ladies' shop when twentieth first signed me in 1948. They were all expensive—one grey, one beige, and one dark blue dress suit."

This portrait from *The Fireball* was taken during a party scene. "Believe it or not," Marilyn said a year later, "I did not own a single cocktail dress until I bought [this] black silk faille dress with a long narrow slit down the front which is held together with a tie. I wore it with black arm-length gloves, and no $125 was better spent in my opinion. Some people thought it was a little daring, but I love the dress." Here, Marilyn has hiked up the mid-calf-length skirt to better expose her legs—in a preview of hemlines to come a decade later.

All About Eve, also in 1950, placed Marilyn in a combination of her own clothes and a studio-designed gown. In the film's famous party scene, she wears a glamorous formal,* but for her brief moments with Bette Davis and George Sanders in a theater lobby, she was once again in her two-toned knit dress, paired this time with her stone martens.

It wasn't financial considerations that led Marilyn to wear her own wardrobe in the lushly budgeted *All About Eve*. It was more a matter of filmmaking exigencies. The production company had only a few days to film at San Francisco's Curran Theater, and no studio wardrobe was available. Monroe gladly agreed to bring her own outfit for this important career boost. Even after she attained superstardom, Marilyn wore some of her own clothes on screen. For *Let's Make Love* in 1960 she was unhappy with many of the designs of Dorothy Jeakins, so she wore things she loved from her personal wardrobe.

*See Charles LeMaire section

SLACKS & JAX

At 6'3", Dan Dailey towers over Marilyn as they pose on the Fox lot in early 1952. When not on public display, Monroe preferred this casual look. She was, after all, a classic Gemini. While some executives at the studio gave her a hard time about her sexy eveningwear, others felt dungarees were too plain for a budding movie goddess.

"The other day," she told *Photoplay* magazine, "When I was hurrying across the lot, wearing blue jeans and a T-shirt I had put on hurriedly at home, I was stopped by one of the executives who told me, 'Marilyn, you shouldn't wear blue jeans on the lot.'

"Why?' I asked, thinking that of all places, the lot was the one place I could feel completely at home.'

"An actress should always look her best,' he said.

"I suppose this is true, but I have always felt comfortable in blue jeans: they're my favorite informal attire. I have found it interesting, however, that people whistle at jeans too. I have to admit that I like mine to fit. There's nothing I hate worse then baggy blue jeans."

(Marilyn can be seen wearing jeans in three films, *Clash by Night*, *River of No Return*, and *The Misfits*).

Darryl Zanuck was often dismayed by Marilyn's unconventional wardrobe choices, but he was a shrewd businessman and he saw a phenomenon in the making. By mid-1952, Marilyn was the most popular star on the Fox lot.

Marilyn dashes through cabin grounds in Banff, Alberta, Canada in the summer of 1953. She is on location for the Otto Preminger western *River of No Return*. The jeans are one of several pairs she wore of selvage denim from Foremost JCP Co., a division of J. C. Penny. These were some of the first Sanforized jeans, guaranteed to suffer minimal shrinkage. This innovation came in handy as Marilyn spent a lot of this movie soaked to the skin after having hundreds of gallons of water flung at her. Around this time she told *Movieland*, "I buy boy's jeans because they're long waisted like me; and boy's shirts go with them."

Monroe and a studio pal share a laugh (over a fountain pen?) in a Fox hallway. Eschewing the usual jeans and T-shirt, Marilyn is in a pretty lounging outfit consisting of a Mandarin collared silk brocade jacket with kimono-style sleeves, a self-tie, and slacks of either silk or gabardine. She has buttoned only one of the three knotted-cord buttons on the jacket. The wedges are in leather with a double instep strap.

Marilyn is captured in 1960 by a photographer hiding outside the Fox studio fence. She is leaving a rehearsal for *Let's Make Love* and is in typical work mode; hair unkempt, wearing casual capris and her blouse tied under her bust. The high heels are the only whisper of glamour.

With another coworker during rehearsals for *The Seven Year Itch*, Marilyn is in a sleeveless, midriff-baring top—with a bra peeking out. The capri pants are so tight they look uncomfortable. Legendary eight-time-Oscar-winning designer Edith Head often said that the one star she regretted never having a chance to design for was Monroe. "Her clothes didn't seem to fit her very well," Head remarked. Many of Marilyn's designers were stymied by her need to keep everything as skin tight as possible.

Producer Buddy Adler appears with Marilyn on January 15, 1960 at the Twentieth Century Fox commissary. They are introducing the press to her *Let's Make Love* leading man, French star Yves Montand.

Simple of line but effective, this dress has a halter-top in pale gray silk jersey. The drop waist leads to a full-length skirt of layered chiffon. The design was originally attributed to John Moore in 1957. He had it fabricated in deep red/orange for Marilyn to wear in sizzling publicity portraits to promote (rather incongruously) *The Prince and the Showgirl*. Marilyn loved the dress and had Moore make one in black.

This version is one of three she had made by Jax. In *Let's Make Love*, Monroe wears a pink version as costar Frankie Vaughn croons "Incurably Romantic," while she moves sensuously behind him. That version, this one from the reception, and another that was Ombrey dyed in gradiating shades of pink* were all carrying a Jax label when Julien's put them up for auction. Most likely, Marilyn took the original Moore design to Jax to duplicate. At the time, Rudi Gernreich was Hanson's newest dressmaker so it is quite possible that these three gowns were the work of Gernreich, then on the cusp of fame.

Jack Hanson, a graduate of Hollywood High School, a World War II vet, and former shortstop with the Los Angeles Angels, was an unapologetic butt man. He thought post-war women's slacks lacked oomph, so he sketched up some ideas, borrowed $500, and opened Jax in the coastal town of Balboa, California. His snug pants zippered up the back, calling attention to the rear end, and they sold for $60 — a hefty amount in the late '50s. Hanson even eliminated hip pockets so nothing would distract from the derriere. Lacking money for advertising, Hanson drew crowds when he had his salesgirls model the line in the shop's window. These were pants that only women with superb shapes dared to wear, but they were a smash and soon he was adding stores in Beverly Hills and New York, near Marilyn Monroe's apartment.

"If any one person made us, it was Marilyn," Hanson told *Sports Illustrated* in a 1967 interview. "She wore our things constantly, everywhere, and was always in the shop. We designed a lot of things especially with her in mind . . ." Hanson and his wife became personal friends of Monroe's, and she encouraged them to add other items to their line. Soon Jax blouses and dresses joined the famous pants. In addition to Monroe, other devoted Jax customers included Natalie Wood, Janet Leigh, Jill St. John, and Nancy Sinatra. Even Audrey Hepburn and Jacqueline Kennedy were rumored to be Jax fans.

*The Ombrey dyed version is now part of the Greg Schreiner collection.

Head to toe in a Jax outfit, Marilyn poses before boarding a plane in early 1962. The silk blouse in a bold black and white print has long sleeves, which Marilyn has rolled up. Her slacks are ankle length, worn with her favorite Ferragamo pumps.

Jack Benny chats with Monroe during rehearsals at Madison Square Garden on May 18, 1962, the day before the birthday extravaganza for John F. Kennedy. Marilyn is in a Pucci blouse and Jax slacks.

SWEATER GIRL

With a wink, a reporter once asked Marilyn, "Why do you look so good in a sweater?" After a moment's thought, she gave as good as she got: "A sweater is like life," she said. "You get nothing out of it that you don't put into it." The quip became part of the Monroe legend. In fact, she had made the most of snug sweaters since elementary school when she developed early and seemingly overnight.

When photographer David Conover first discovered Norma Jeane working the assembly line at the Radio Plane Parts Company, he wanted to take her outside for a few shots. "Don't you have a sweater?" he asked. "I mean, in your locker?" "Sure," she said, "I always have a sweater." From that first modeling session on, Monroe and sweaters proved a winning combination.

In the spring of 1949, with no movie work in her immediate future, Marilyn kept her face and figure before the public by accepting any publicity opportunity that came along. Here on May 18, she poses on a miniature loveseat at the annual Pacific Antiques Show at the Pan Pacific Auditorium in Los Angeles. The exuberant Monroe smile that would become world famous is in full force as she fills out a pair of khaki-colored gabardine shorts and an off-white angora pullover.

fucking perfect.

A year later, she poses in a sporty turtleneck for a portrait to promote *Hometown Story*. As with all the clothes she wore in the film, this was from her own closet. She also wore it for *Asphalt Jungle* publicity. Marilyn, of course, chose to emphasize her figure by adding a belt, though it wasn't required. This style made a comeback in the mid-1970s, when it would be worn over a long-sleeved shirt for a layered look.

Marilyn most likely bought the sweater at Orbach's department store in the Miracle Mile area of Wilshire Blvd. The store featured the sweater prominently in newspaper ads of the time. It was a popular design that even turned up on Ethel Mertz of all people. Vivian Vance wore it on Episode #24, in the first season of *I Love Lucy*.

The summer of 1953 found Marilyn in Banff, Alberta, Canada to shoot locations for *River of No Return*. The crisp temperatures gave her a chance to show off a variety of sweaters during breaks in filming. Here she poses in a white cable knit pullover with ribbing on the turtleneck and midriff.

SWEATER GIRL

This short-sleeved pullover is in black wool.

One warm afternoon, Monroe agreed to a pinup sitting that resulted in this lovely pose. The white ribbed-knit top features peasant knit trim and was a rather ordinary style until Marilyn pulled it off her shoulders. She combined it with an unusual pair of high-waisted shorts in a black stretch knit. Her stripped wedges were a favorite pair of casual shoes.

Naturally, not every sweater Marilyn wore was chosen for maximum sex impact. For an afternoon of cycling at London's Windsor Great Park in August 1956, she wore classic sportswear: a cardigan in navy with ribbed cuffs

On the set of *Let's Make Love* in 1960, Marilyn is in the midst of shooting "My Heart Belongs to Daddy," her opening number. She is wearing the most famous of her on-screen sweaters. It is oversized in cashmere cable knit imported from Dublin by Dorothy Jeakins, Monroe's designer on the production.

Marilyn snuggles against a cool morning on the beach at Santa Monica in the summer of 1962 for photographer George Barris. The sweater is a self-belted cream wool bulky knit cardigan embellished with a bold brown geometric pattern at the collar, across the center, and at the cuffs.

The prior February, Marilyn and her housekeeper/companion Eunice Murray were shopping in Toluca, Mexico for furnishings for Monroe's new Brentwood home. In 1975 Murray recalled that Marilyn noticed a stack of the sweaters in a little shop where they were handmade and said, "I can wear these on chilly mornings when I have to leave the house early."

The Barris photos of Monroe in the sweater weren't published until Norman Mailer included one in his popular book on Marilyn in 1972. When Marilyn's fans saw the Barris photos they became fascinated by the sweater. They tracked down the maker and began ordering so many that he had to hire extra help. Because it tied like a bathrobe, the sweater could be worn by members of either sex and this, coupled with its cheap price, made a hugely popular import within a couple of years. Several Mexican firms began producing versions. By the mid-'70s, it was a ubiquitous fashion among young people, who wore the sweater over T-shirts and funky jeans. It remained a wardrobe staple until the early '80s. A variation of the sweater received huge exposure in the late '70s, when it was worn by Paul Michael Glaser in the hit TV series *Starsky and Hutch*. With her whimsical sense of humor and democratic social views, Marilyn would surely have enjoyed the fact that she instigated this unexpected fashion craze, not for a glamorous Hollywood creation, but for an inexpensive *schmatte* that could be worn by anyone.

PHOTOGRAPHY CREDITS

Associated Press Photo: pages 194, 197, 227

Baron/Pix: pages 176, 177

Carl Perutz © Pete Livingston: cover, pages 213, 224

Cecil Beaton/Sotheby's Belgravia: page 83

Collection of Keya Morgan/Lincolnimages.com: pages 11, 77, 79, 211

David Conover: page 17

Earl Moran/Playboy Enterprises: page 248

George Barris: pages 119, 273, back cover

George Zeno Collection: pages 8, 9, 12, 13, 15, 19, 20–23, 25, 27, 29, 30, 33, 37–41, 43, 44, 46–49, 51–55, 57–60, 61(bottom), 62 (right), 64, 65, 67, 69, 70–76, 78–81, 85, 87–97, 98 (bottom), 99, 104, 107, 109, 110–113, 116–118, 120, 121, 123–129, 131–134, 137–164, 166–173, 175, 178–181, 183, 185, 186 (left), 187, 189, 192, 193, 195, 196, 198, 199, 201, 202, 204–208, 210, 214–221, 225, 228 (right), 229–231, 234, 239, 243–245, 247, 250–252, 255–259, 262, 263, 265–269, 271

Hollywood Press Syndicate: page 260

Hyman Fink/*Photoplay*: page 135

International News Photos: pages 101, 102, 237, 242

J. R. Eyerman/Getty: page 249

Lawrence Kronquist/FPG: page 18

London Daily Express: page 290

Los Angeles Examiner: page 61

Lou Valentino Collection: page 203

Metropolitan Photo Service Inc.: page 182

Milton Greene/Legends: page 86

Mirror Pic/*Daily Mirror*: page 235

Paul Popper/European Photos: page 263

Paul Schumach: page 31

Philippe Halsman/Magnum: page 34

Photoworld/FPG: page 45

Pictorial Parade: page 130

Pierluigi/Pix: page 98

Richard Avedon/Warner Bros.: pages 4, 7, 105

Sam Shaw/Rex: page 241

Scott Fortner: page 261

United Press Photo: pages 35, 36, 62, 63, 90, 95, 103, 106, 115, 191, 209, 228, 239, 240

Wide World Photo: pages 102, 186

INDEX

A

Academy Awards, 42, 50, 56, 58, 68, 108, 122, 136, 157, 161
Actor's Studio, 84, 96–97, 100
Adler, Buddy, 260
Adventures of Don Juan, The, 136
Aguilera, Christina, 12
All About Eve, 56, 57–58, 134, 238, 253
American in Paris, An, 108
American Weekly, 212–213
Ames Brothers, 147
Anello & Davide, 235
Anthony, Ray, 45
"Anyone Can See I Love You," 69
Arden, Elizabeth, 82
Arlen, Roxanne, 171
As Young as You Feel, 123, 125
Asphalt Jungle, The, 20, 202–203, 238, 266–267
Astaire, Fred, 203
Avedon, Richard, 105

B

Baby Doll, 104
Bacall, Lauren, 157, 160, 209
Bachelor Flat, 171
Bacon, James, 155
Baker, Gladys, 16
Balenciaga, Cristobal, 90
Ball, Lucille, 50, 68, 122, 212
Bardot, Brigitte, 236
Barnhart, Sylvia, 19
Barris, George, 118–120, 272

Barrymore, Drew, 204
Bass, Walter, 176
Bates, Barbara, 134
Battelle, Kenneth, 116, 209, 210
Beatles, The, 235
Beaton, Cecil, 83, 84
Belafonte, Harry, 79
Benny, Jack, 79, 227, 263
Benson, Sam, 156
Bergman, Ingrid, 42
Berlin, Irving, 68, 165
Best, Marjorie, 136
Big Combo, The, 64
Blackwell, Earl, 79
Blue Book Model Agency, 18
Bogart, Humphrey, 160
Brando, Marlon, 163
Brooks, Rand, 214
Brown, Kay, 86
Brown, Wally, 123
Bullocks Wilshire, 177
Bus Stop, 173, 178

C

Calas, Maria, 79
Call Me Madam, 152
Cambridge, Duke and Duchess of, 114, 173
Carey, Mariah, 40
Carnegie, Hattie, 68, 100, 244
Carson, Jack, 162
Casablanca, 108
Cashin, Bonnie, 183
Cassini, Oleg, 10, 26–31
Cat on a Hot Tin Roof, 102
Chapman, Ceil, 32–41, 100, 133

Charisse, Cyd, 75, 210
Chierichetti, David, 157
Chouinard Art Institute, 50, 136
Christie's auction, 72, 77, 121, 158, 228
City Club, 215
Clash By Night, 23, 129, 256
Cleopatra, 122
Clift, Montgomery, 74, 95
Club Del Mar, 27
Coburn, Charles, 153
Cold Shoulder, 250
Conley, Renié. *see* Renié
Conover, David, 16–17, 264
Conte, Richard, 250
Conversation Piece, 41
Copeland, Joan, 41
Cornered, 128
Cortese, Valentina, 58
cosmetic surgery, 20
Coty Awards, 82, 100, 209, 234
Coward, Noel, 41
Cox, Dorothy, 175
Crain, Jeanne, 222
Cramer, Richard Ben, 68
Crawford, Joan, 68, 155, 157, 180, 236
Crist, Judith, 84
Curtis, Tony, 94, 113

D

Dailey, Dan, 165, 256
Dallas, 155
Dalrymple, Jean, 77
Davis, Bette, 108, 253
Davis, Viola, 155

Dawson, Beatrice, 235
Day, Doris, 68, 176
Day the Earth Stood Still, The, 136
Dean, William F., 36
DeHaven, Gloria, 58
DeMille, Cecil B., 160
Desirée, 163
"Diamonds Are a Girl's Best
    Friend," 148–149, 150–151, 152
Dick Tracy, 161
Dick Van Dyke Show, The, 176
Dietrich, Marlene, 64, 77
DiMaggio, Joe, 36, 60–61, 63, 68,
    103, 120, 141, 171, 186, 205, 228
Dior, Christian, 227
Dishonored Lady, 50
Donatello, David di, 97
Don't Bother to Knock, 139, 238
Doubt, 155
Dougherty, James, 191
Dunne, Irene, 68

E

East of Eden, 180
Eisenhower, Mamie, 212
Ekberg, Anita, 236
El Morocco, 63
Elizabeth (Queen), 77, 234, 235–237
Etherington-Smith, Meredith, 12, 177
"Every Baby Needs a Da-da-
    daddy," 70
Ewell, Tom, 167
Eyman, Scott, 180

F

Ferragamo, 10, 262
Fireball, The, 207, 250–253
5,000 Fingers of Dr. T, The, 228
Flanagan, Agnes, 207, 210

Fleming, Victor, 42
Fonda, Jane, 56
Foremost JCP Co., 257
42nd Street, 108
Four Jills in a Jeep, 64
Francis, Anne, 193
Frank & Joseph's salon, 19
Freed, Arthur, 64
Funny Girl, 64

G

Gable, Clark, 71, 74, 97, 98, 208
Gage, Ben, 63
Galanos, James, 230, 234
Garland, Judy, 209
Gaultier, Jean Paul, 8, 171
Gaynor, Mitzi, 165
Gentlemen Prefer Blondes, 48,
    137, 144–147, 150–151, 153,
    158, 161, 200–201, 216
George Raft Story, The, 113
Gernreich, Rudi, 176, 261
Gigi, 83, 92
Gilda, 68, 249
Girl Next Door, The, 161
Glaser, Paul Michael, 272
Golden Globe Awards, 106–107,
    194, 210
Grable, Betty, 157, 161
Grant, Cary, 140–141
Grauman's Chinese Theatre, 16, 48
Greene, Amy, 86, 100
Greene, Milton, 100, 180
Greer, Jane, 58
Guilaroff, Sidney, 203, 207
Gunther Jaeckel, 182

H

Hale, Alan, Jr., 250
Halsman, Philippe, 35, 94

Hansford, Andrew, 136
Hanson, Jack, 261
"Happy Birthday," 10, 78–79,
    210–211
Hargitay, Mickey, 155
Harper's Bazaar, 114
Hartnell, Norman, 234
Haver, June, 161
Hayworth, Rita, 68, 249
Head, Edith, 26, 50, 58, 259
Hefner, Hugh, 142
Heim, Jacques, 131
Henaghan, Jim, 191
Henie, Sonja, 136
Henrietta Awards, 27
Hepburn, Audrey, 9, 114, 176,
    209, 261
Hero's Life, A (Cramer), 68
Hill, Craig, 131
Hoffman, Alice, 60
Holiday, Judy, 68
Hometown Story, 250, 266–267
House on Telegraph Hill, The, 58
Hover, Herman, 131
How To Marry a Millionaire, 55,
    156, 157–161, 196, 216
Hurley, Elizabeth, 155
Huston, John, 71, 203
Hyde, Johnny, 20

I

I Love Lucy, 50, 64, 267
I. Magnin's department store, 42,
    238–239, 244
"I Want To Be Loved By You," 113
Irene, 182

J

Jack Benny Show, The, 161
Jax, 118, 120, 245, 260–263

Jeakins, Dorothy, 10, 42–49, 50, 231, 253, 271
Jenssen, Elois, 50–55
Jessel, George, 20
"JFK dress," 77–79, 80
Joan of Arc, 42
Johnson, J. Seward, Jr., 173
Johnson, Lady Bird, 82
Johnson, Lynda Bird, 210
Joseph Magnin's, 60–61
Journal American, 44

K

Kamm, Herbert, 87
Karinska, Barbara, 42
Kaye, Danny, 30
Kelley, Tom, 22, 173
Kelly, Gene, 98
Kelly, Grace, 9, 176
Kennedy, Jacqueline, 26, 75, 82, 104, 209, 210, 261
Kennedy, John F., 10, 77, 78–79, 104, 210, 263
Khrushchev, Nikita, 98
Kirk, Lisa, 82
"Kiss," 45
Knef, Hildegard, 156
Korea trip, 36–38, 40, 217
Krasner, Milton, 57

L

Ladies of the Chorus, 22, 69–70, 212, 214
Lady in the Dark, 64
Ladyship Gowns, 32
LaMarr, Barbara, 56
Lang, Fritz, 64
Lansbury, Angela, 82
Lassie, 45
Lawford, Peter, 78

Lawrence, Gertrude, 68
LeBrock, Kelly, 171
Lee, Peggy, 79
Leigh, Janet, 261
Leigh, Vivian, 232–233
LeMaire, Charles, 10, 56–63, 156, 157, 222
Lemon, Jack, 94
Les Girls, 108
Let's Make It Legal, 131, 134
Let's Make Love, 42, 49, 94, 98, 173, 194, 231, 253, 259–261, 271
Lewis, Jerry, 40
Life, 35
Lincoln, Abraham, 240
Lollobrigida, Gina, 114
Loper, Don, 64–67, 100
Lopez, Jennifer, 114
Loren, Sophia, 114
Louis, Jean, 10, 49, 68–81, 225
Louis-Dreyfus, Julia, 171
Love Happy, 22, 247
Love Nest, 126–127, 132–133, 220–221
Lundigan, Billy, 126

M

MacDonald, Jeanette, 203
MacLaine, Shirley, 79
Madonna, 12, 114, 151, 161
Magnani, Anna, 97
Mailer, Norman, 272
Maltese Falcon, The, 108
Manor-Bourne line, 244
Mansfield, Jayne, 12, 32, 155
"Marilyn," 45
Marilyn Monroe Productions, 102
Martin, Dean, 40, 75, 98
Marx, Groucho, 22, 247
Masters, George, 194, 210
"Material Girl," 151

Mature, Victor, 236–237
Maxwell, Elsa, 104
McKee, Grace, 16
McMullen, 175
McQueen, Alexander, 8
Merman, Ethel, 156, 165
Metropolitan Museum of Art, 82
Middleton, Kate, 173
Miller, Arthur, 41, 74, 82, 86, 97, 104, 182, 187, 194, 205, 223, 229, 232–233, 235, 242
Miller, Isidore, 77
Minnelli, Liza, 203
Miracle, Berniece, 77, 90, 131
Miranda, Carmen, 235
Mirisch, Walter, 90
Misfits, The, 49, 70–73, 80, 95, 207, 225, 245, 256
Miss America Pageant, 35, 53, 142
Miss Piggy, 171
modeling, 16–19
Mo'Nique, 171
Monkey Business, 31, 138, 140–141
Montand, Yves, 98, 260
Moore, John, 49, 82–99, 180, 187, 229, 232–233, 260
Moore, Mary Tyler, 176
Moran, Earl, 249
Morgan, Jane, 236
Mortenson, Edward, 16
Moulton, Thomas, 58
Movieland, 16
Mr. John, 212, 216
Mr. President, 68
Mugler, Thierry, 8, 155
Murray, Eunice, 272
Murray, Wayne, 72, 181
Mussolini, Benito, 114
My Fair Lady, 83
"My Heart Belongs to Daddy," 49, 271
My Week with Marilyn, 12

N

Nardiello, George, 178, 180–181
Newcomb, Pat, 183
Newman, Joseph M., 131
Niagara, 42, 44–47, 125, 161
Nichols, Barbara, 113
Night of the Iguana, The, 42
Nilton, Nicky, 32
Norell, Norman, 82, 100–107,
    161, 180–181, 209
North, Sheree, 155
Northridge, Laddie, 212–213, 224
Novak, Kim, 68
nude photographs, 22, 142, 149,
    173

O

O'Connor, Donald, 165
Olivier, Laurence, 84, 232–233
Ombrey, 261
*On a Clear Day You Can See
    Forever*, 83
On the Riviera, 30, 31
Orry-Kelly, 108–113
Osbourne, Kelly, 12
Oscars. *see* Academy Awards
Otis Art Institute, 42

P

Paget, Debra, 58
Pantages Theatre, 58
Paris Follies of 1956, 64
Parker, Richard, 210
Parsons, Louella, 41, 209
Parsons School of Design, 82,
    180
Pearson, Albie, 81
Perry, Katy, 171

Peters, Jean, 125
Photoplay, 153–155, 238
Playboy, 71, 142
Powell, Dick, 128
Powers, Mala, 131
Pratt Institute, 100
Preminger, Otto, 27, 257
Presley, Priscilla, 155
Prince and the Showgirl, The, 84, 87,
    97, 229, 232, 235, 236, 260
Principal, Victoria, 155
Private Secretary, 50
Pucci, Emilio, 114–121, 231, 263
"Put the Blame on Mame," 68

Q

Quinn, Louis, 155

R

Rancho Notorious, 64
Rasmussen, Gladys, 161, 197
Ray, Johnny, 165
Reagan, Nancy, 234
Réard, Louis, 131
Renié, 58, 122–135, 220
Rettig, Tommy, 228
Rex of Beverly Hills, 212
Reynolds, Debbie, 144, 171, 173
Rhodes, Leah, 136
River of No Return, 205, 219, 228,
    256–257, 267
Roach, Hal, 136
Rogers, Ginger, 64, 68, 122
Rooney, Mickey, 45, 250–251
Roosevelt, Eleanor, 212
Russell, Jane, 48, 144–147, 216
Russell, Lillian, 28
Russell, Rosalind, 68
Russell, Theresa, 171

S

Samson and Delilah, 50
Sanders, George, 253
Savani, Nick, 131
Schlesinger, Arthur, Jr., 79
Schreiner, Greg, 46, 169, 261
Seven Year Itch, The, 9, 63, 71,
    100, 103, 166–173, 186, 191,
    198–199, 259
Shakira, 12
Sharaff, Irene, 122
Showgirl, 236
Sinatra, Frank, 72, 98, 106
Sinatra, Nancy, 261
Skolsky, Sydney, 135
Skouras, Spyros, 126
Slightly Dangerous, 203
Smith, Anna Nicole, 12
Smith, Liz, 12
Smithsonian Institution, 82
Smurfette, 171
Snively, Emmeline, 18–19
Snow White, 122
Snows of Kilimanjaro, The, 156
Snyder, Alan "Whitey," 161, 196
Solid Gold Cadillac, The, 68
Some Like It Hot, 41, 90, 93–94,
    97, 108–113, 182, 194, 196,
    207, 209, 243–244
Something's Got to Give, 74–75,
    98, 212, 218
"Sooner or Later," 161
Sothern, Ann, 50
Sound of Music, The, 42
"Specialization," 94
Spirit of St. Louis, The, 155
St. John, Jill, 261
St. Laurent, Yves, 8
Starsky and Hutch, 272
Steele, Gile, 50
Stefani, Gwen, 12
Steinem, Gloria, 116

Stevenson, Adlai, 79
Strasberg, Lee, 97, 100
Strasberg, Susan, 116
Streisand, Barbra, 64, 171
subway scene, 170–173, 240
    see also *Seven Year Itch, The*
Summer, Donna, 171
Summers, Anthony, 100
Swanson, Gloria, 100

T

Take Care of My Little Girl, 222
Talmack, Mattie, 82
Taylor, Elizabeth, 32
Temple, Shirley, 136
Ten Commandments, The, 42
"That Old Black Magic," 173
There's No Business Like Show Business, 156, 163–166
Thorpe, Jay, 212
Three Stooges, The, 122
Tierney, Gene, 26, 27, 30
Travilla, William, 136–173, 185
Tron, 50
Turner, Lana, 203
"Two Little Girls from Little Rock," 144–145

U

U.S.O., 36–37

V

Vale, Nina, 128
Valentino, 155
Valentino, Rudolph, 100
Van Cleef & Arpels, 102
Van Doren, Mamie, 32
Vance, Vivian, 267

Vanderbilt, Gloria, 32
Vaughn, Frankie, 261
Vélez, Lupe, 122, 136
Versace, Gianni, 118
View from the Bridge, A, 235

W

Wakeling, Gwen, 50
Warhol, Andy, 142
Watts, Naomi, 155
Way We Were, The, 42
Wayne, David, 216
We're Not Married, 50–52
Where the Sidewalk Ends, 27
Wild Is the Wind, 97
Wilder, Billy, 113
Williams, Esther, 63
Winchell, Walter, 199
Windsor, Duchess of, 68
Wood, Natalie, 261

Y

Yolanda and the Thief, 203
Young, Loretta, 68, 157
Young Frankenstein, 42

Z

Zanuck, Darryl F., 238, 256
Ziegfeld Follies, The, 56
Zolotow, Maurice, 126, 196

ACKNOWLEDGMENTS

The authors first wish to acknowledge three people who went above and beyond in contributing to this project:

Dhona M. Spacinsky, designer and founder of *donajean, inc.*, professor of design and textiles at Academy of Couture Art, associate of FIDM and the Art Institute of Los Angeles, MFA; Cal State University. Dhona's enthusiasm and sense of humor were a delight and her knowledge essential.

Renaissance man Greg Schreiner was always available to the authors despite the demands of his busy life. He is the proprietor of The Marilyn Monroe Site online, a producer of musical revues, and an accomplished pianist. He allowed access to his impressive collection of Monroe costumes and costume sketches, and graciously shared his extensive knowledge about the construction of film costumes.

Wayne Murray of Design Resource is second to none in his knowledge of mid-century design houses, fabrics, and styles. He is also a relentless researcher, leaving no page of stacks of vintage fashion magazines unturned in his quest for accuracy.

We are grateful also for the help of Monroe wardrobe aficionado and photographer, Scott Fortner and to Andrew Hansford for sharing information about his book subject, William Travilla.

Further thanks go to Alfred Arena, Bobbie Baker Burrows at Life Books, Carl Berg, Paul Breskick, Ben Carbonetto, David Friend, Judy Greenberg, Arnold Horton, Alma Torres Lee, Christina Leiberman, Howard Mandelbaum at Photofest, William Mann, Richard Nicholson, Andrew Powell, Robert Scott, James Spada, Adam Surangsophon, Karen Swenson, Lou Valentino, Vilma Zeno, the helpful staffs of the New York Public Library and the Margaret Herrick Library at the Academy of Motion Picture Arts and Sciences, and Doris Raymond, vintage clothing maven and proprietor of The Way We Wore in Los Angeles

For their support, encouragement, and in some cases, love—we are very grateful to William Arabatzis, Randy Brown, Frank Burton, Robert Cullen, Peter Cervi, James Farrell, Patrick Gordon, Nicholas Gunn, David Hamilton, Paul Ivy, Tim Newth, Clint, Heather, and Hunter Nickens, Mike Parente, Richard Parker, Merry Shiels, Judy and Eileen Spinner, Billy K. Tyler, Guy Vespoint, and Michael Vigilante.

The authors must also thank our editor, Cindy DeLa Hoz, for her perseverance and patience, and our designer, Corinda Cook, for her discerning eye and enthusiasm. Finally, a nod to *Project Runway* for episode five of season three, in which Marilyn Monroe was featured as an inspirational fashion icon—which in turn inspired the notion of this book.

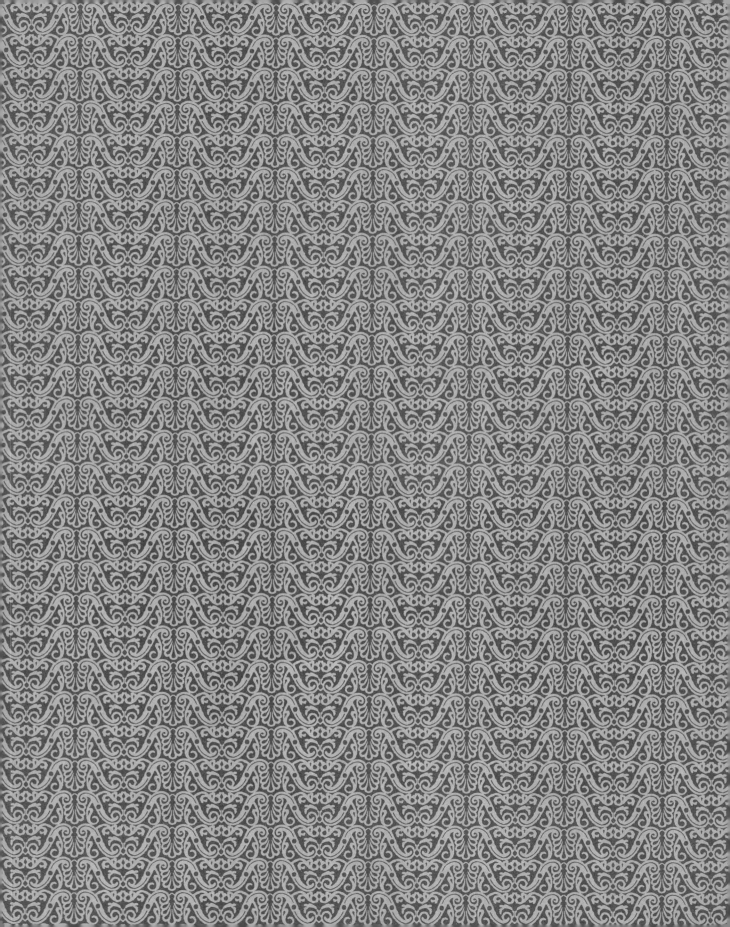